ONE-MINUTE MEDITATIONS
FOR BUSY PEOPLE

One-Minute Meditations
for Busy People

REV. JOHN H. HAMPSCH, C.M.F.

CHARIS

Servant Publications
Ann Arbor, Michigan

Charis Books is an imprint of Servant Publications designed to serve Roman
Catholics.

Published by Servant Publications
P.O. Box 8617
Ann Arbor, Michigan 48107

Cover design by Hile Illustration and Design, Ann Arbor, Michigan

96 97 98 99 00 10 9 8 7 6 5 4 3 2 1

Printed in the United States of America
ISBN 0-89283-957-0

Library of Congress Cataloging-in-Publication Data

Hampsch, John H.
  One minute meditations for busy people / John H. Hampsch, C.M.F.
    p.   cm.
  "Charis."
  ISBN 0-89283-957-0
  1. Meditations.   2. Devotional calendars.   I. Title.
BX2182.2H34 1996
242—dc20   96-4563
                                     CIP

CONTENTS

INTRODUCTION

Cats are smart. In some ways they're smarter than humans. Unlike us, cats—with rare exceptions—will not overeat, even with food always available to them. In contrast, we humans tend to eat too much at one sitting—a major cause of overweight. Scientific nutritional studies have revealed that "nourishing nibbling," to prevent mealtime gluttonizing, is a healthful way to lose weight.

Our spiritual nourishment, like bodily nourishment, is best taken by appropriate "snacks," rather than by inordinate gorging. Significantly, the Latin word for wisdom, *sapientia*, is derived from *sapere*, meaning to taste or savor with delight. Spiritual gourmets, who are graced with true wisdom, have learned to "savor" God's goodness in his revealed truth, not by glutting themselves but by enjoying the divine haute cuisine, relishing each *bonne bouche* of his banquet table, one morsel at a time.

The delight of "relishing" or "savoring" God's revealed word is the essence of meditation: "Blessed is the one... whose delight is in the law [word] of the Lord, and on his law he *med-itates*" (Ps 1:2). *One-Minute Meditations for Busy People* is an attempt to proffer Scripture-flavored "nourishing nibbles" for anyone—even those who are not "busy." Whether used as a bedside book (for midnight snacking), or as snappy weekday homily material for priests, or as anybody's "food for thought," my prayerful wish is:

Bon appétit!

Sinner's Story—It Could Be Verse

In a moment of levity, I dashed off the following ditty:

> *Peter thrice denied the Lord; Zacchaeus was a cheat;*
> *And then there was the prostitute who wept at Jesus'*
> *   feet.*
> *Simon was an anarchist, Matthew plundered taxes;*
> *The "sons of thunder," James and John, were angry*
> *   battle-axes.*
> *Paul, a rabid terrorist, and Dismas was a thief;*
> *Magdalene was demon-filled, and Thomas lacked*
> *   belief.*
> *But there they are in heaven, smiling down upon us*
> *   now;*
> *Each wears a brilliant halo tilted on a battered brow.*
> *So things for us are looking up, in this salvation*
> *   business—*
> *No matter what our "was-ness" was, what truly*
> *   counts is "is-ness."*

Somehow it's consoling to know that Jesus began his ministry by shepherding a ragtag flock of black sheep to work with him. "My power," the Lord revealed to Paul, "is made perfect in weakness"—to which Paul reacted, "For Christ's sake, I delight in weaknesses… for when I am weak, then I am strong" (2 Cor 12:9-10). In that paradox he saw the source of power of many Old Testament heroes, whose weaknesses were turned to strengths (see Hebrews 11:34).

It is consoling to know that when we are discouraged and overwhelmed by our own spiritual weakness and ineptitude, God isn't discouraged with us. It is then that we should say, "I can do everything *through him* who gives me strength" (Phil 4:13).

Mountain That's Never Been Seen

2

Did you know that the world's second highest mountain has never been seen by human eyes? A few feet lower than Mount Everest, it's *twice* as tall as the highest mountain in the continental United States. Discovered in 1953 by oceanographers sonar-mapping the Pacific ocean floor, the pinnacle of this 28,500-foot mountain lies 1,200 feet below the ocean's surface—rising from the ocean bottom in the Tonga Trench between New Zealand and Samoa.

Many of the earth's greatest wonders lie hidden and unrecognized. Likewise, many awesome wonders of the human soul lie submerged, unrecognized, and for the most part tragically unused and unappreciated, such as the stupendous capacity of human love. Exceptions include the great saints whose mystical experiences have lofted them to the dizzy heights of love-union with God while immersed in the ocean of his tenderness. They feebly strive—and fail—to articulate the experience of these ineffable encounters, amazed that they even survived them.

For such love experts, Scripture scintillates with meaning: "I have loved you with an everlasting love; I have drawn you with loving-kindness" (Jer 31:3). And beyond life lie yet more unseen mountains of God's love: "No eye has seen, no ear has heard, no mind has conceived what God has prepared for those who love him" (1 Cor 2:9); "Neither height nor depth... will be able to separate us from the love of God" (Rom 8:39). God's love is lovely. Immerse yourself!

How to Outrun a Deer

Imagine hunting a deer by simply running after it until it drops dead of exhaustion! The incredible Tarahumara Indians—the world's fastest and most indefatigable runners—do just that in the rugged mountains of southern Mexico. Swilling bat blood with dried turtle meat, trainees are kept awake by deer-hoof rattles at their belts, pursuing wild horses on foot for as long as three days. Children, kicking wooden balls over a sixty-mile course, engage in foot races lasting six to eight hours. A nonstop run of one hundred seventy miles is a typical adult practice session. Tribal messengers, pacesetters that make Olympic athletes look like cronies, run the narrow steep mountain trails from Guazapares to Chihuahua and back in five days—a distance of over six hundred miles!

Such prodigious feats of endurance are, of course, beyond the physical capacity of most of us. But spiritually, with grace-nourishment, our soul-capacity is even more amazing. While we "run... to get the prize,... a crown that will last forever" (1 Cor 9:24-25), remember, "the race is not to the swift" (Eccl 9:11), but to those who *persevere*. This prize goes only to those who "throw off everything that hinders and the sin that so easily entangles, and... run with perseverance the race" (Heb 12:1).

An Easy Way to Make It Rain

4

Would you believe that it's possible to make it rain by simply demanding it with a loud voice? It's true! High in China's Gaoligong Mountains in the northwest part of Yunnan Province are a group of pools nicknamed "The Enchanting Lakes." When anyone shouts for rain while standing near the lakes, a downpour often immediately follows, says the *Shanghai Liberation Daily*. The louder the shout, the heavier the rain; the longer the shout, the longer the rain.

To explain this believe-it-or-not phenomenon, physicists theorize that the air around the lakes is often supersaturated with humidity, which precipitates as rain when coalesced by certain vibrations, such as a high-volume or high-pitched voice.

We have all fantasized of getting instant response to our heaven-directed prayers, like tourists inducing rainfall by bellowing near the Enchanting Lakes. After all, Jesus did say, "Whatever you ask for in prayer, believe that you have received it, and it will be yours" (Mk 11:24). But if the belief (faith) requirement is defective, the spiritual "vibes" will be inadequate.

The solution? Two sentences before the above quote, Jesus says, "Have faith *in God*." It is only when we exert God-oriented faith that this *promise* will be effective. Mere faith in our faith or faith in our prayer is not enough to do the trick.

Amnesty Day

The Chicago Public Library recently declared an "Amnesty Day" for borrowers of overdue books. With no fines and no questions asked, over ten thousand books were returned, some overdue since 1934!

Every day is "Amnesty Day" with God; he's more eager to forgive us our debts than we are eager to be forgiven. "You are forgiving and good, O Lord, abounding in love to all who call to you" (Ps 86:5). Who would not call on him? Who more than a prisoner enjoys freedom? And who more than a sinner should enjoy God's forgiveness? Since everyone is a sinner (see 1 John 1:8) we can all rejoice that for us, forgiveness is incredibly easy, since "the blood of Jesus... purifies us from all sin" (v. 7).

For the return of an overdue sinner, no questions will be asked; just return to God in humble repentance. Any Magdalene can hear the gentle, forgiving voice of Jesus urging her to sin no more. A dying thief can hear the promise of an immediate paradise. The housewife with her peccadillos of impatience can feel the soothing balm of Christ's tender mercy. The inconsiderate husband sees his selfishness replaced by the selflessness of a strong but kindly Jesus. The child sees his little flaws of disobedience melt in the springtime smile of the lover of little ones. No questions asked, but the ear of God is always attuned to hear the sheepish words, "I'm sorry," as we "approach the throne of grace... to receive mercy" (Heb 4:16).

6

Instead of paying a fine for your next traffic violation, how would you like to write your own obituary? Or would you prefer to interview an undertaker, or perhaps view the bodies of traffic victims in the local morgue? An alternative might be to spend a few hours in a hospital emergency room, viewing injured patients.

These are some of the "fines" imposed on young traffic violators by a judge in Gary, Indiana. This dramatic approach has reduced teenage accidents from three hundred a week to only about twenty-five—a mere twelfth of the former average! In a newspaper interview, the judge remarked: "When they bring in their obits and reports, the kids are very chastened. It's a terrible, sobering experience for them. They learn to foresee consequences."

If we could foresee the consequences of our failings, we would indeed be chastened. A vision of hell would shock the most inveterate sinner into fervent conversion. Saints given visions of purgatory quickly learned to avoid even apparently insignificant failings. If we could see, with a "God's-eye view," the effect of the cooling of our love for God, it would startle us. Yet, it is perhaps more challenging not to see these things, for "blessed are those who have not seen and yet have believed" (Jn 20:29).

Instead, try pondering the words of Sirach 7:36 (NAB): "In everything you do, remember your last days, and you will never sin."

How Much Is a Human Worth?

At mid-century prices, an iron ingot sold for $5. Made into horseshoes, its value was $10.50. Manufactured into needles, its value jumped to $5,000. Crafted into high-grade balance springs for watches, it's worth a quarter of a million dollars!

Workmanship of a human enhances the value of the most ordinary material. But what is the value of the human workman, "made... a little lower than the heavenly beings and crowned... with glory and honor" (Ps 8:5)? The decline of morality, according to James Reston, is due to the "decline in the belief in each person as something precious." Value-regard is the soil of love—the criterion by which all men will know that we are Jesus' disciples (see John 13:35). The challenge is to "not love [merely] with words or tongue but with actions and in truth" (1 Jn 3:18).

There are countless ways to do this: a father devoting as much time and interest to his wife and children as to his job; a mother radiating inspiration, as only she can, to her children; a student studying diligently to be better prepared to change the world by his chosen profession; the nurse who shows that the "unwritten ingredient in each prescription is love"; the mechanic who enjoys making cars safer for others; the politician who puts truth and justice above the garnishing of votes; the writer who seeks to uplift, not downgrade, the ideals of his readers; the "everyman" who cultivates love wherever it isn't thriving.

Hot Spot Where Fleas Freeze

8

If you're hankering for an unusual vacation, visit Mount Raupehu, the loftiest rise on New Zealand's North Island. This nine thousand-foot mountain is a semi-active volcano with a sixty-acre crater lake nestled in its peak—a steaming lake of *hot* water surrounded by walls of solid ice and snow! Too hot to swim in, the lake is used by tourists for boating amid surrounding snow peaks.

Only intense heat rising from the volcanic core could keep the water hot in an otherwise frigid atmosphere, where not even hardy insects can survive. Similarly, only a soul continuously warmed by ardent love of God can maintain its fervor in a worldly atmosphere of icy selfishness, greed, lust, and pride, where Christ is ignored or all but forgotten. Jesus warns that in the end times, "because of the increase of wickedness, the love of *most* will grow cold, but he who stands firm to the end will be saved" (Mt 24:12-13).

Only a disciplined life of prayer, sacrifice, and devout reception of the sacraments can protect us against the cooling of our enthusiasm for things of God. The Lord's warm compliment for our devotion is counterpointed by his cool warning, as with the early Christians at Ephesus: "You... have endured hardships for my name, and have not grown weary. Yet I hold this against you: You have forsaken your first love.... Repent and do the things you did at first.... To him who overcomes, I will give the right to eat from the tree of life, which is in... paradise" (Rv 2:3-7).

Ignorance Is Not Bliss

A priggish little old lady inquiring about a European tour was told by the travel agent that one particular tour included the famous Oberammergau Passion Play. Misconstruing the word "passion" she indignantly exclaimed, "I'm tired of all this sex stuff; and now it's even featured as a travel highlight! Shame on you!" With that, she stormed out of the office.

"Ignorance has something to be said for it," Mark Twain once quipped, "It gives rise to about nine-tenths of the world's conversational output." But certainly much ignorance fits into the moral category of "inculpable" or "invincible" ignorance. Jesus refused to consider anyone a sinner who acts in ignorance; the soldiers crucifying him were ignorant of his divinity, so he prayed, "Father, forgive them, for they do not *know* what they are doing" (Lk 23:34).

Many times we do not know the evil we're doing, but even when we are aware of it, we can still in a way remain ignorant—ignorant of how much we are loved by God, in spite of our sin. If we knew of God's awesome love for us, how differently we would act!

Ignorance of God's love for us leaves us in a kind of spiritual darkness. Jesus, asking his Father to pardon his executioners on the basis of ignorance, intimates that this "darkness"—that of not knowing the gift of God's love—is a sad deprivation. Let us be always ready to let his love shine brightly in our souls.

Condition for Fission

10

The same type of energy that makes the sun and stars burn for countless centuries is known to reside in prodigious quantities in every tiny drop of sea water. The challenge is to find a way to release that stored energy.

Every high school student learns in science class that potential energy must be converted to kinetic energy before it can produce any physical change or motion. Thus, gasoline must be combusted by a spark in the engine's piston chamber before it can move a car. Likewise, a soul must be grace-sparked before it can grow in holiness and earn merit or heavenly reward. God provides the spark ("prevenient grace"), "for it is God who works in you to *will* and to *act* according to his good purpose" (Phil 2:13). But that spark of grace can be quenched by our noncooperation before it can produce its God-intended effect.

Like the gargantuan energies hidden in a drop of sea water, enormous spiritual energies lie hidden and untapped in our soul. Our resolve to cooperate with grace in the release of the Spirit's power within can bring astonishing and world-changing effects.

Please Don't Be Seated

O n a tour of a palace in Austria, weary from jet lag and endless walking, I longed to sit down in any chair I could find. But every chair in the palace was obviously a precious antique, richly embroidered and exquisitely upholstered. The very ornateness of the furniture seemed to forbid me to be seated.

A sense of unworthiness in the presence of great opulence is perhaps normal for one not accustomed to such luxury. Yet I suppose one could grow to feel more at home if one actually inherited such a mansion and lived in it. I'm sure we won't feel so awkward and uncomfortable and out-of-place in our splendid celestial mansion—our heavenly inheritance that Jesus is now preparing for us. "In my Father's house are many rooms…. I am going there to prepare a place for you…. I will come back and take you to be with me that you may be where I am" (Jn 14:2-3).

Yet your sense of unworthiness in the presence of God himself will probably never diminish, for it is nothing more than profound reverence in the awesome presence of the Almighty. "I, by your great mercy, will come into your house; in reverence will I bow down" (Ps 5:7). This would be fearful in itself, if that reverence did not entail an awareness of his incredible love for each of us that will excite our love in response. As earth-tourists on a wearying pilgrimage, let us anticipate resting in his embrace!

12

The antenna on the atomic warhead at Hiroshima that signaled the bomb's detonation altitude was made—of all places—in Japan. Similarly, much of Iraq's weaponry employed in the Gulf War originated in America. War is replete with such ironies.

But so is spiritual warfare. Sin has a way of boomeranging on us with a vengeance. Just as "the nations have fallen into the pit they have dug," warns David, "… the wicked are ensnared by the work of their hands" (Ps 9:15-16).

In no form of evil is this self-poisoning more evident than in the sins of resentment, bitterness, and unforgiveness. The resentful person has a greatly heightened risk of several types of disorders, especially cardiovascular disease, report the researchers at Duke University Medical Center. We would do well to heed Paul's warning: "Get rid of all bitterness, rage and anger,… along with every form of malice,… forgiving each other" (Eph 4:31-32).

In the ominous words of Proverbs, "If a man digs a pit, he will fall into it; if a man rolls a stone, it will roll back on him" (Prv 26:27). The ancient Chinese proverb says it even more pithily: "If you would bury your enemy, dig two graves."

Ways to Read God's Love Letter

Ohe of the things that motivate cultural archaeologists to keep digging deeper after making a find is the realization that many ancient cities are "stacked" on the ruins of previous cities; often several civilizations are found at the same location.

Likewise, exploring God's word, we discover levels of truth. *Historical truth*—facts or words involving real people and events—often lead to *doctrinal truths* about God, man, sin, and salvation. Digging deeper, we find *practical truth*, enabling us to act on God's word (see James 1:22-25), where learning leads to living. And even deeper probing reveals *devotional truth*, where the Holy Spirit teaches us (see John 14:26; 15:26; 16:13-15) through his sacred words in ways that enlighten, enable, enrich, and encourage us.

God's word was not written *to* us but *for* us (see 2 Timothy 3:16). Digging through that word at the deepest level—that of devotional truth—we focus on the spiritual essentials, not on geographical or historical incidentals. For instance, prayerful meditation on the miraculous opening of the Red Sea (see Exodus 14) may remind us of the many times God has "opened up" opportunities for us in difficult situations. Have we ever thanked him for those grace-filled opportunities?

Prayerful reading of God's word can warn us (see 1 Corinthians 10:1-12), offer hope to us (see Romans 15:4), and provide many other helpful insights, especially as we come to recognize it as a personal message from him (see 1 Thessalonians 2:13).

Exhale and Hearty

14

An amazing breath analyzer developed in Columbus, Ohio, can diagnose various diseases by detecting specific chemicals in a patient's breath. Dimethyl sulfide indicates liver disease, amines are linked to lung cancer, diabetics breathe out acetone, and heart-disease persons show traces of pentane. Researchers soon hope to be able to detect colon cancer and other deadly diseases, as well as air pollution in homes and workplaces, with this simple and painless technique.

Like a human body, a diseased soul, riddled with sin habits, gives off indicators of the disorder within. A hope-weak person breathes out an aura of depression or negativity. A hate-filled, resentful person radiates rancor and rebellion. An impatient person is upset by even mild adversities. A lustful person cannot long conceal sexual innuendoes or a subtle acting out of lascivious fantasies. A vain or prideful person shows egocentric behavior or speech. An uncharitable person is a fountain of gossip, slander, or detraction. Each sin-habit "breathes out" its own form of poison.

In its original etymology, the word spirit means "breath." "Bad breath" would show a bad spirit within. Diagnosing the reported behavior of the Corinthians, Paul suspected that they were diseased with "quarreling, jealousy, outbursts of anger, factions, slander, gossip, arrogance and disorder" (2 Cor 12:20). We might check our breath every so often. We may need more than mouthwash.

A Li'l Dab'll Do Ya

Typical spider silk, of which cobwebs are composed, is stronger than steel of the same thickness. Yet a single strand of this webbing, if it were long enough to stretch all the way around the world, would weigh less than a pound.

For some things, a little goes a long way, like the microscopic portions of trace minerals such as phosphorus or magnesium, that are needed to maintain cardiovascular health. A little virtue in a God-focused person goes a long way, too, for the Lord is "able to make all grace abound to you, so that in all things at all times, having all that you need, you will abound in every good work" (2 Cor 9:8).

Our God is a God of the hundredfold, whose return to us far exceeds the little we give him. He promises that "a good measure, pressed down, shaken together and running over, will be poured into your lap" (Lk 6:38). Paul reminds us that the Lord "is able to do *immeasurably more than all we ask or imagine*, according to his power that is at work within us" (Eph 3:20).

A simple act of love of God, an interior act of humility, a tiny effort to be patient, a love-motivated act of courtesy will cause him to tug you close to his heart and grace-kiss your soul. As the old hair cream commercial put it, "A li'l dab'll do ya!"

16

A team of *Reader's Digest* editors staged a country-wide test of honesty by "losing" 120 wallets in public places in twelve U.S. cities. Each wallet contained $50 in cash along with a name, local address, and phone number; coupons; notes; and family photos. Surveillance teams noted behavior patterns of each "lucky" finder. Surprisingly, two out of three of the wallets were returned intact to the "owner." Some finders even refused the offer of a $50 reward.

Two conclusions were derived from the experiment: First, even dishonest people have a functioning conscience. The furtive glances and attempts at concealment observed in the dishonest finders indicated that they knew they were doing wrong. "A sense of shame is not a bad moral compass," wrote General Colin Powell.

The second conclusion: The conscience is refined primarily by moral training in one's childhood. Most of the honest finders, when interviewed, said that their desire to do the morally right thing had been instilled in them early in life by their parents. "Train a child in the way he should go," says God's word, "and when he is old he will not turn from it" (Prv 22:6).

In the blunt words of General H. Norman Schwarzkopf, "One always knows the right thing to do. The hard part is doing it." Yet, those who seek God's help are promised sufficient strength to resist temptation (see 1 Corinthians 10:13).

God's Waiting Room

One of the more ironic terms in our frenetic world is the term "rush hour"—the hour when drivers "rush" into a frustrating near-gridlock. Similarly, in our prayer life, our urgent "please-rush" prayer petitions often meet with only exasperating delays.

We are often in more of a hurry than God is. Peter, sinking into the water, prayed hastily and urgently, "Lord, save me!" David's panicked prayer in Psalm 70 is another example: "Hasten,... O Lord, come quickly to help me.... O Lord, do not delay." (Apparently he had forgotten his own advice in Psalms 27:14: "Wait for the Lord; be strong and take heart and wait for the Lord.")

In times like these, where is God, who promises to give "grace to help us *in our time of need*" (Heb 4:16)? Faith answers: God's timing orchestrates his loving providence; "The Lord is a God of justice. Blessed are all who *wait* for him" (Is 30:18).

Joseph waited two years to be freed from prison. His patience paid off, enabling him to reconcile with his family and save many lives (see Genesis 50:19-21). Moses waited through ten plagues and forty years of desert heat. Mary and Martha watched Lazarus die while waiting for Jesus (see John 11). If you're in a hurry when God isn't, synchronize your watch with his. His delays are neither denials nor defeats, but merely his providentially disguised love.

18

"**U**p until now my health has been excellent," said an elderly lady to her husband. "I wonder if I'll live to be a hundred?"

"Not if you stay thirty-nine much longer," he retorted.

Regardless of our age, we should periodically take a "rearview mirror" inventory of our life up to the present, as well as a "windshield view" of the future, as David did in Psalm 71. Recalling his trust in the Lord from his infancy through his youth (vv. 5 and 6), he showed a resultant rare adolescent docility (v. 17). And his "windshield view" of his advancing age entailed zeal-fired plans to extol God's greatness to the next generation (v. 18). His agenda admitted of no "rocking-chair retirement" on that score.

This psalm offers a God-centered retirement plan for all of us: ongoing prayer (v. 3), continual praise (vv. 6 and 8), and continual hope (v. 14), rather than complaints of aches and pains with petulant nostalgic longing for the "good old days." Depending on the Lord's strength as our own grows weak (v. 15), we can use every opportunity to witness for him (v. 16)—which becomes a heart-song of love.

Those who love deeply never grow old. They may die of old age, but they die young—knowing that the best is yet to come.

How's That Again?

Following the Battle of Waterloo, a ship off the south coast of England began to relay to London the news of Napoleon's defeat. A dense fog settled in just as the first two words of the semaphore were decoded from the top of Winchester Cathedral: "Wellington defeated..." All Londoners were heart-broken—until the fog lifted and the sentence became fully visible: "Wellington defeated the enemy!"

Frequently our discouragement comes from not *really* listening to the constant messages the Lord sends to us. We must truly listen with our hearts—and keep listening until his entire message gets through, whatever way it is communicated. "My sheep listen to my voice," said Jesus—and his voice is uttered in many ways: through our conscience, through the Church, through the good example of others, or through a gentle inspiration of grace.

Jesus is always there to guide and support us. "He is able to help those who are being tempted" (Heb 2:18). This is especially true when we're tempted to discouragement during trials and hardships, when it *seems* the Lord has forgotten us. He is there! He is always there, even when we're asleep and not thinking of him (see Psalm 139:18). Whenever we are discouraged, we can be sure that we lack awareness of his loving presence and guiding support.

20

In Cincinnati, more than a century ago, an artist who was also a chess expert painted a picture of Satan apparently checkmating a hopeless-looking young man. Of the hundreds of chess players that viewed the painting, only one detected a possible loophole strategy on the painted chessboard that could leave Satan defeated. He convinced the aging chess champion, Paul Morphy of New Orleans, to come to Cincinnati and study the painting. Within a half hour of conjectured planning, Morphy devised a combination chess move that would have defeated the devil in the painting.

"Snatching victory from the mouth of defeat" was an experience of Jesus' disciples, when, after a grueling night of drawing up empty nets, they felt hopelessly defeated—until Jesus shouted from the shore, "Throw your net on the *right* side of the boat." Following this simple suggestion, they caught so many fish, they couldn't haul their nets aboard! (see John 21:6). Their apparent defeat exploded into victory, and the difference was only a boat width—from port to starboard! With Jesus' guidance, success is often right at our fingertips!

When we feel exhausted and defeated by the enemy, victory may be very close, be it a healing, a solution to a problem, or an answer to prayer. Heeding Jesus' loving guidance from the sideline enables us to snatch victory from the mouth of defeat, for "we are more than conquerors through him who loved us" (Rom 8:37).

The gentle love conveyed by a gold-set diamond engagement ring sharply contrasts with tremendous upheaval associated with the ring's origin. Diamonds are simply carbon, super-heated and super-squeezed in the roots of a volcano—conduits called "kimberlite pipes." Silver, copper, and even gold are also spawned by volcanoes. (The Antarctic volcano Mount Erebus, when erupting, dusts the white continent with microscopic particles of pure gold.)

Gold and diamonds are expected to last "forever"—just as every couple expects their love to last. However, the sad fact remains that such tender honeymoon love, if not carefully and prayerfully cultivated, can easily erupt into fiery marital arguments that spew forth a lava of resentment and bitterness. The "diamond" character of either spouse, or both, may not prove to be shatterproof, and the "fool's gold" of love may tarnish with boredom, daily routine, and repeated inconsiderateness so common in Christ-less marriages. Such are the countless sad cases that clog our divorce courts.

True "gold-and-diamond" love is Scripture-piloted, so that the husband is challenged to seek, earnestly and self-sacrificially, the wife's happiness and holiness (Eph 5:25), and is "won over" by the reverent submission of his wife (see 1 Peter 3:1.) Today is a good day for a Bible-based assessment of your marriage.

A Friend Who Doubles Your Joy and Divides Your Sorrow

22

That astute wordsmith, Samuel Johnson, wisely advised, "Keep your friendships in good repair." There's hardly any conceivable life situation in which a close friend is not an asset. In the anguish of bereavement or in the exulting joy of celebration, the presence of a loyal and loving friend is a treasure, while the absence of a friend at such events is an unthinkable privation.

"You are my friends," Jesus joyfully proclaimed. "I no longer call you servants, because a servant does not know his master's business.... I have called you friends, for everything that I learned from my Father I have made known to you" (Jn 15: 14-15).

It's easy to overlook the tremendous implications of this privilege of having Jesus for a personal friend to whom we can turn with total confidence for this divine guidance and security in our every undertaking, as he "makes known to us everything he has learned from his Father." And to think he is only a whisper away!

His friendship becomes more meaningful if we cultivate it. We can do this by opening ourselves to the very thoughts of God through the Spirit of Jesus, "that we may *understand* what God has freely given us" (see 1 Corinthians 2:11-12). With this precious "knowledge of his will through all spiritual wisdom and understanding" (Col 1:9-10), we can daily grow in the knowledge of God. Let us listen more than speak to our friend. He has so much to tell us!

With All Your Heart—
Art of the Big-Hearted

The heart of a blue whale, caught in 1947, was hoisted onto a giant scale. It registered an amazing 1,540 pounds! The heart of this world's largest animal seems awesome to us, but the really big-hearted are the human love champions that love their enemies.

Jesus spells out his command (not option) for us to love our enemies, not just our friends. "Do good to those who hate you, bless those who curse you, pray for those who mistreat you" (Lk 6:27-28). He even says we must "lend to them without expecting to get anything back. Then your reward will be great" (v. 35).

Such "hard sayings" of Jesus, like "forgive *from your heart*" (Mt 18:35), are scales that measure how big our heart is, and also whether we can truly call ourselves Christians: "If you hold to my teaching, you are really my disciples" (Jn 8:31). And, "By this all men will know that you are my disciples, if you love one another" (Jn 13:35).

It's hard enough to love an irksome fellow worker or a neighbor who lets his barking dog annoy you. Even in cases of serious hurts and injustices, it is possible to love, but only if we realize that we are not required to *like* our enemies, but to have "benevolent" love for them—that is, to *desire good* for them. That big-heartedness is mega-Christianity!

24

Clocks move clockwise because they were modeled after the shadow movement of the gnomon on sundials. (You knew that, didn't you?) But did you ever wonder why horse races, dog races, auto races, and human track races all run counterclockwise, as well as skating rinks and carousels? Dance pupils told to take a "warm-up walk around the room" tend to circle counterclockwise. This "time-reversal instinct," according to some psychologists, is simply a subconscious desire to run back away from the oncoming locomotive—death.

Job saw time as "but a shadow" (Jb 8:9). Time and time again, God's word reminds us that time is lent to be spent, directly or indirectly, in the Lord's service. "Be very careful, then, how you live," says Paul, "not as unwise but as wise, making the most of every opportunity" (Eph 5:15-16). Ralph Waldo Emerson echoed that thought: "Any time is a good time if you know what to do with it."

The Bible affirms that our lifetime (not just the time of our life) is short and uncertain. And we must "render an account of our stewardship" of that time loan. Above all, time is precious. In Ben Franklin's words, "If time be of all things most precious, wasting time must be the greatest prodigality." Think about it!

Did you hear about the nearsighted porcupine who was hospitalized when he mistook a cactus for his sweetheart?

Except as joke material, myopic porcupines are a rarity. But among humans, myopia is not uncommon—especially spiritual myopia. A surprising number of things we observe every day are distorted in our mind; our more "farsighted" outlook is impeded by what psychologists call "selective perceptivity." When this happens, we subconsciously filter out some of the discomfiting elements of reality, such as many good aspects of God's providence, and also distasteful aspects of our failures.

Thus, an escape from a near disaster may not be seen for what it is—an intervention of divine providence—but simply as a "close call" or "stroke of luck." Or a breathtaking scene of a colorful sunset or snowcapped mountain may be admired without "seeing" its source—a loving Creator. Like toddlers at Christmas, we may "myopically" focus on the gift while ignoring the giver.

Evil, too, may be distorted. Abortion may be euphemized as a mere "termination of pregnancy" rather than as a heinous act of infanticide. Adultery regarded as a merely innocuous "affair." "The eye is the lamp of the body," said Jesus. "If then the light within you is darkness, how great is that darkness!" (Mt 6:22-23). Let our prayer be that of the blind man: "Lord, I want to see!"

26

Every culture has its own particular gestures for specific meanings—some of which may seem strange to us. But one of the few body language gestures that anthropologists recognize as being common to all nationalities and tribes on earth is the tossing upward of the hands as an expression of frustration. It's a sign of letting go, giving up—a "what's-the-use?" sort of gesture.

While globally common to all cultures, this simple shrug of defeat is never used by persons with an iron-jaw character who are always determined to persevere against all odds.

Authentic perseverance is a virtue, not to be confused with stubbornness, which is merely unreasonable intransigence. "Do not harden your hearts," God's word advises (see Hebrews 3:8,15). George Santayana observed that: "A fanatic is one who redoubles his effort when he loses sight of his goal." Christian (God-focused) perseverance is a derivative of the virtue of fortitude, and will be especially important for the end times. "He who stands firm to the end will be saved," Jesus reminds us in all the synoptic gospels. "By standing firm you will gain life" (Lk 21:19).

Let us practice perseverance in all its forms: in faith (Col 1:23), in confidence (Heb 3:6, 14), in doctrine (2 Thes 2:15), in unity (Phil 1:27), in tribulation (Rom 12:12), and in love (1 Cor 13:7).

It Ain't Heavy—It's Just a Cross

A typical commercial plane can carry about 1.3 times its own weight in passengers and luggage. But, aerodynamically speaking, a dragonfly is superior; it can easily flight-lift seven times its own weight.

When the burdens of life weigh us down, we may feel at times that we are carrying far more than our own weight. From the time of Christ, society has given a name to these burdens—they're called crosses. Even before Jesus carried and died on his own cross, he told his followers, "If anyone would come after me, he must deny himself and take up his cross daily and follow me" (Lk 9:23).

In citing that classic passage, often overlooked is the word "daily." For most, it is not too hard to put up with even a heavy burden for a short while. But on our long "transcontinental" flight from here to eternity, long-term hardships—that is, the "daily," ongoing troubles—can be truly wearisome. And yet, the heavy weight seems to decrease as one's strength increases with daily perseverance.

Every burden-wearied person can find strength-restoring rest in loving intimacy with Jesus: "Come to me, all you who are weary and burdened, and I will give you rest. Take my yoke upon you and learn from me,... and you will find rest for your souls. For my yoke is easy and my burden is light" (Mt 11:28-30).

28

"**A** great many people believe they are thinking when they are merely rearranging their prejudices." Only a philosopher-psychologist like William James could have formulated that bit of wit.

Even the Pharisees and Herodians admitted that Jesus was unprejudiced and a man of integrity (Mt 22:16). But we ordinary humans cannot altogether make that claim for ourselves. Everyone has preconceived ideas that originate from one's culture or environment.

According to Scripture, showing partiality to one person or group is sinful (see James 2:9). And yet, adhering to a divinely revealed truth is not a "prejudice" but a God-supported command "to keep... instructions without partiality" (1 Tm 5:21). If, as Jesus said, the truth shall make us free, it is by freeing us from prejudice that would dilute the truth.

Jesus promised, "The Holy Spirit... will teach you all things and will remind you of everything I have said to you" (Jn 14: 26). One task of the Spirit of Jesus is to immunize us against prejudice.

Traffic That Can Drive You Mad

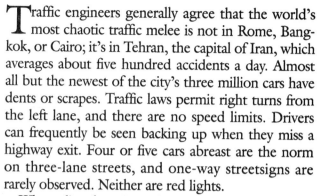

Traffic engineers generally agree that the world's most chaotic traffic melee is not in Rome, Bangkok, or Cairo; it's in Tehran, the capital of Iran, which averages about five hundred accidents a day. Almost all but the newest of the city's three million cars have dents or scrapes. Traffic laws permit right turns from the left lane, and there are no speed limits. Drivers can frequently be seen backing up when they miss a highway exit. Four or five cars abreast are the norm on three-lane streets, and one-way streetsigns are rarely observed. Neither are red lights.

Where disorder reigns, disaster flourishes, but God desires that "everything should be done in a fitting and orderly way" (1 Cor 14:40). Like disorderly traffic, moral conduct in disarray results in widespread disaster: "Where you have envy and selfish ambition, there you find disorder and every evil practice" (Jas 3:16).

Some of those disorderly practices, says Paul, include: "sexual immorality, impurity and debauchery; idolatry and witchcraft; hatred, discord, jealousy, fits of rage, selfish ambition, dissensions, factions and envy; drunkenness, orgies, and the like.... Those who live like this will not inherit the kingdom of God" (Gal 5:19-21). Other lists of such vices that reflect disorder in souls, and in society at large, are found in 1 Corinthians 6:9-10, Ephesians 5:5, and Revelation 22:15. Most of these disorders involve a disturbed relationship toward others, just as traffic problems are often the result of disregard of the rights and welfare of others. When we can all learn to love and respect others consistently, we'll have a happier and safer world.

30 It is now known that Picasso, early in his career, used many of his drawings as kindling in his room stove on chilly days. Today those drawings would be worth a king's ransom.

It is often only in retrospect that we see the great value of things we have allowed to slip through our fingers. Perhaps our moment of most poignant awareness (and regret) will be the moment after death, when God "will reward each person according to what he has done" (Ps 62:12; see Romans 2:6). In that moment we'll see countless lost opportunities for growth in holiness and consequent merit (eternal heavenly reward). Every tiny opportunity to do good—which is irretrievable if unused—entails an occasion for growth in holiness as well as its promised hundredfold reward.

"Anyone who gives… a cup of water in my name… will certainly not lose his reward," promised Jesus (Mk 9:41). Offering a cup of water is a nearly insignificant act of kindness, but when done *in his name*, it produces a reward to be enjoyed, not for a hundred years or a million, but for eternity!

Why the disproportionate reward? Jesus gives the answer in Matthew 25:34-40: "You who are blessed by my Father; take your inheritance, the kingdom prepared for you,… [for] whatever you did for one of the least of these brothers of mine, *you did for me.*" A get-well card or an act of traffic courtesy, a cheerful "Good morning!" or preparing a family meal: These pebbles of human kindness will be transformed into gemstones in the treasuries of heaven!

Fire Power

About 200 million years ago—give or take 10 or 20 million—when the proto-continents of Africa and North America snuggled together with no Atlantic ocean between, Casablanca would have been a suburb of New York City. The present geography was wrought by an intense seismic reaction sixty miles beneath the surface. The resulting heat produced a sea of semi-molten material that enabled the continents to float apart.

There is another fire that is designed to "renew the face of the earth." It's the fire that Jesus spoke of with such ardor: "I have come to bring fire on the earth, and how I wish it were already kindled!" (Lk 12:49). As his subsequent remarks indicate, his proclamation of the kingdom is a refining and purifying fire. His message is inflammatory because it is controversial—a source of conflict and dissension even within families. It will separate not continents, as done by the subterranean fiery magma, but vast throngs of those who accept and those who reject him, as a smelter separates the dross from the metal. John the Baptist spoke of the "burning of the chaff" when separated from the wheat (see Matthew 3:12).

For us the bottom line is the challenge of Jesus: "He who is not with me is against me, and he who does not gather with me scatters" (Mt 12:30). The choice is really a series of countless choices, almost moment by moment, in every situation in which our love for God is put to the test. St. Augustine provided a reliable shibboleth for choosing: "Love God and do whatever you want."

Crocodile Tears

A "laughing hyena" doesn't really laugh, of course: its yelp is a sound that resembles strident laughter. Nor does a crocodile shed tears of grief while consuming its prey, though this ancient belief has spawned the phrase that connotes insincerity. Nature is replete with such counterfeit behavior patterns, but so is super-nature—the supernatural life that we are called to live.

One form of such fakery is a false kind of contrition or sorrow for sin, to be clearly distinguished from the real thing, as Paul asserts. "*Godly sorrow* brings repentance that leads to salvation and leaves no regret, but worldly sorrow brings death" (2 Cor 7:10). God isn't primarily interested in mere apologies: he wants us to experience a sin-remorse that results in a different attitude and a change of behavior (*metanoia*) that involves not just a stopping of sin but a turning to God in sincerity of heart.

Godly sorrow is supported by the Holy Spirit's power, enabling us to change in three ways: It gives strength to resist future temptation, it makes us less arrogantly self-assured of our own efforts toward holiness, and it makes us more God-dependent. This "repentance unto life" (Acts 11:18) is not mere dread of punishment, but love-sparked "perfect contrition," so dear to God.

Without genuine humility in a heart broken not only for sin but also *from* sin, tears of sorrow are merely crocodile tears.

Heaven's Hidden Treasure

A pious shipbuilder in Holland by the name of Peter Jansen reasoned that the basic design for the ark as revealed by God to Noah should be an ideal blueprint for such vessels. So he built a smaller ship of the same proportions—six times as long as wide, and with the height one-tenth of the length. Disregarding the ridicule heaped upon him in the course of the construction, like Noah himself, Jansen found that the completed ship could carry one third more freight, would sail faster, and was safer than the old type ship. Today, with minimum variations, this design is used for almost all modern freighters.

Studying the word of God has opened up exciting vistas for archaeologists, historians, paleographers, linguists, geologists, and geographers, not to mention theologians. But even more significantly, by prayer, not just study, the word of God has enriched countless thousands of persons with awesome spiritual insights reserved for those who prayerfully learn to "read between the lines" of his great love letter, the Bible.

Countless nuggets of wisdom still remain to be quarried from the gold mine of God's inspired word by Spirit-sensitive persons. At each discovery, they exalt with the psalmist: "I rejoice in following your statutes as one rejoices in great riches,... like one who finds great spoil.... The unfolding of your words... gives understanding to the simple" (Ps 119:14, 162, 130). Decide today not to neglect this fathomless treasure right at your fingertips.

34

Without punctuation, many writings and utterances would be meaningless gobbledygook. As an example, try to make sense of this unpunctuated series of words: "That that is is that that is not is not is not that it it is." But with proper punctuation added, those same words read: "That that is, is; that that is not, is not. Is not that it? It is."

The human life, unpunctuated by faith, is meaningless. In his book *Believing*, Eugene Kennedy states, "Faith is closely linked to a person... and related to his whole identity. There is no believing that does not involve the whole person. You cannot give a response of faith with only a part of your personality."

Compare an agnostic's experience of bereavement with that of a faith-filled individual who believes in an afterlife. Compare a faithless person's reaction to an insult with that of a Christian with a stalwart faith that has learned to turn the other cheek. Compare a worldling's frustration in sustaining intractable pain with the pain of a true believer, soothed by the loving acceptance of God's will in suffering. Compare an atheist's enjoy-it-while-you-can hedonism with the joy of the friend who attends the bridegroom with a joy that is "complete" (see John 3:29). Truly, only faith-punctuation can put real meaning into otherwise meaningless situations in life.

"Yes, Lord?"

There's a two-word epitaph on a small and inexpensive headstone of a lad buried in an obscure country cemetery in England. The words are: "Freddy!"—as if someone had called the boy's name—and underneath, as if the boy had answered, was the one-word question-response: "Yes?" That simple dialogue epitaph epitomized the virtuous life of a youth who early on had learned to respond promptly and lovingly to God's will.

This nearly unknown hero reminds me of another young lad who learned, with Eli's help, to respond to the call of God. "Speak, Lord, for your servant is listening," was Samuel's answer to the call of the Lord (see 1 Samuel 3:9). But it was only after three bewildering calls that he learned to discern the Lord's voice. Becoming sensitized to it is a somewhat protracted learning process; it takes time for a sheep to become sensitized to hear and recognize the shepherd's voice (see John 10:4). But ours is a truly patient Shepherd; he calls our name (with whispers rather than shouts) and waits for our "Yes?"

As our sensitivity grows, we learn not only to hear the whispered calls of the Lord but also to "answer the phone" more promptly. His whispers may come as subtle inspirations of grace, gentle leadings in prayer, or enticements to passionate gratitude. Once the grace-response habit is established, we learn to connect with God on a deeper, more constant level. "Pray continually," admonishes the Apostle Paul. "Give thanks in all circumstances, for this is God's will for you in Christ Jesus" (1 Thes 5:17-18).

Saved by the Bell

36

The phrase "saved by the bell" does not come from boxing, as most people think, but from seventeenth-century guards at Windsor Castle. Any sentry caught asleep on duty incurred the death penalty. One thus-accused sentry protested his innocence, stating that he had heard the bell in the clock tower of St. Paul's Cathedral strike thirteen times at midnight. The tribunal doubted him, until witnesses attested that in fact on that evening the defective clock had tolled not twelve but thirteen times. Thus he was "saved by the bell."

Being suspect or falsely accused is an experience that few escape in life. Old Testament luminaries like Job, Joseph, Moses, and David suffered from it. Even Jesus was no exception; neither was Mary (see Matthew 1:19). Stephen (see Acts 6:11) felt its sting, as did Paul and Silas (see Acts 16:20-21) and countless saints and martyrs, as well as the ancient prophets (see Matthew 5:12). "No servant is greater than his master," said Jesus. "If they persecuted me, they will persecute you also" (Jn 15:20).

Jesus proposes a triple challenge in facing false accusations: First, regard it as a blessing: *"Blessed* are you when people insult you, persecute you and falsely say evil against you." Second, do not merely tolerate it, but rejoice in it, "because *great* is your reward in heaven" (see Matthew 5:12). Third— and here is the real hitch!—we must *pray* for our persecutors (see Matthew 5:44), asking God to bless them (see Romans 12:14). A triple saint-making challenge!

Loving Makes You Lovable

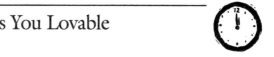

The ennobling pattern of love fascinated the probing mind of a great Spanish philosopher, José Ortega y Gasset. Love, he said, "consists in the constant beaming forth of a favorable atmosphere... a light in which we envelop the beloved, so that all his or her good qualities can reveal themselves. (Hatred, on the contrary, puts the hated person in a negative light, so that we see only his defects.) Love rearranges the possible perfections of the beloved, making us see what we would not see without it."

Like a polarizing lens that cuts the distracting glare from our view, authentic Christian love of a person, while not denying that individual's human weakness, puts it aside so that the basic beauty, dignity, and nobility of the person can shine through. For such a lover, the beloved is seen in the polarized Christ-light of the Gospel: "As the Father has loved me, so have I loved you.... Love each other as I have loved you" (Jn 15:9, 12).

God's divine love-light, polarized through Jesus, is to be prismatically filtered through each of us to each other. Only by this divine light can we see the divine features in all those made to his image and likeness. His vertical love is meant to be spread horizontally through us as human love in any sinless form. As we loan God our hearts to love others, his own goodness in them becomes patent. This is truly an intoxicating experience!

Hair of the Dog

38

An ancient Roman belief was that "like cures like." Thus, as a remedy for a dog-bite the victim would attach to his skin a patch of hair from the dog that bit him. From this evolved the modern version of "hair of the dog"—"curing" a morning-after hangover from a drinking binge by taking a stiff drink.

Without the superstitious implications, it can be said that divine providence has chosen to follow a kind of "like cures like" pattern in remedying mankind's hangover from the original sin—the sin-binge of our proto-parents in the Garden of Eden. That disastrous human failure called for a "human" remedy—a human person who could represent fallen humanity before God, but one who would also be divine, in order to atone adequately to the divine majesty that was offended. Both requirements were fulfilled in our God-man Redeemer, as the second chapter of Hebrews explains.

Because his incarnation was completed through his suffering (see Hebrews 2:10), the "like cures like" principle is not limited to his redeeming us, but is extended even to our physical healing; even our suffering can be "cured" by his. Peter (see 1 Peter 2:24) reasserts this by quoting Isaiah: "By his wounds we are healed" (Is 53:5).

Admittedly, this approach to healing—"dumping" on the Lord our sufferings, knowing that he has already borne them for us—requires a consummate and rare form of faith. Let us ask for it.

Gradual Relapse, Sudden Collapse

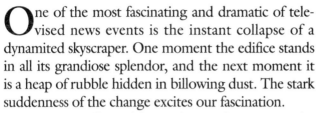

One of the most fascinating and dramatic of televised news events is the instant collapse of a dynamited skyscraper. One moment the edifice stands in all its grandiose splendor, and the next moment it is a heap of rubble hidden in billowing dust. The stark suddenness of the change excites our fascination.

But is it really sudden? The implosion was the result of a long and detailed preparation of the building's interior by the demolition crew, with strategically planned sequenced explosions.

John 13 tells of the collapse of two apostles, Judas and Peter. Judas' betrayal of Jesus is not too surprising, since it was a prolonged and deliberate plan. But Peter? How could this ardent disciple, the first pope, curse and thrice deny his Lord within minutes, even after hearing Jesus prophesy to that effect? *Any* devout but careless soul, "pre-ignited" by the "flaming arrows of the evil one" (Eph 6:16), can suddenly collapse.

Satan and his "familiar spirits" are familiar with each one's particular areas of weakness; he knows where to place the dynamite charges. David's weakness was a lust for Bathsheba; an entire generation paid for it. Peter, after boasting that he would even die for Jesus, still "leaned on his own understanding," contrary to Proverbs 3:5. Ponder often the words of Paul: "If you think you are standing firm, be careful that you don't fall" (1 Cor 10:12). The only assurance we have of not falling is derived from unwavering trust in the Lord.

40

Among ancient warring Anglo-Saxons, the guarding of the community's bread supply from enemy pilfering was critical to survival. The "hlaf-weard" or "load ward" was a trusted "loaf-keeper." The term was contracted to "hlaford," and in Middle English, evolved into "laferd," "loverd," and finally into a later English word "lord"—a master of household supplies. It was then ennobled as the English translation of the Latin "dominus."

It is perhaps more providential than coincidental that Jesus, who acknowledged for himself the title "Lord" (see John 13:13), was born in Bethlehem, which means the House of Bread. He who taught us to ask for our daily bread acted as the divine "loaf-keeper," even multiplying five loaves to feed five thousand, and using the occasion to urge us to seek a far better bread that he would provide—one that endures to eternal life. In that same chapter he referred to his very self as the "bread of God" (Jn 13:33), and repeatedly as the bread of life: *"This bread is my flesh, which I will give for the life of the world"* (v. 51).

"There is only one thing God doesn't know," teased St. Augustine. "He does not know how he could give us a gift greater than himself—and he has given us himself as bread in the Holy Eucharist." This thought-provoking insight should entice us to yearn for this "Bread of God" with the hunger-prayer of that early audience: "Lord, give us this bread always!" (Jn 6:34, RSV).

God's Test of Silence

Is it by coincidence or design that the word "silent" is an anagram of the word "listen"—that is, they both have the same letters? Good listening begins with silence on the part of the listener, but in God's paradoxical ways, one can also be made a good listener by silence on the part of the "speaker" or revealer.

The Lord's silence in refusing to respond to Job's pleas for an explanation of his agonies was probably more severe than the very sufferings that gave rise to those pleadings; certainly his pain was a test, but even more so was his supposed abandonment by God, who responded to his cries with apparently cruel silence.

In doing this, the Lord was not trying to convey his attitude toward Job, but to elicit from Job an awareness of his own petty attitude of petulance toward God. In other words, God's silence was a painful but enlightening *test* which Job flunked in some way. Finally enlightened, he apologized for complaining (see Job 42:6).

Is not God's silence merciful in not having revealed to you ten years ago the sufferings you have endured since that time? Could you have faced such sufferings if he had shown you at that time a preview of them? Wasn't God merciful in not having answered your prayer request to heal a sick relative, when you couldn't understand that death itself, as a door to eternal bliss, was a much better healing than a physical healing for that person at that time? Only an incandescent faith can see merciful love in God's silence.

God's Silence of Disapproval

42

Can you recall the childhood scene of a raised eye-brow, or a tight-lipped silence of your mother or father in response to your juvenile misbehavior? Such silence spoke louder than a verbal rebuke; it clearly communicated an act of judgment.

By just such an act of silent communication God often expresses his displeasure with us when we don't live up to his love-cushioned demands. Eleven centuries before Christ, the priests at Shiloh, Eli's sons, "were treating the Lord's offering with contempt," and "in those days [the century marking the period of the Judges] the word of the Lord was rare" (1 Sm 2:17; 3:1). It will happen again amidst the end-time evils, when "men will stagger from sea to sea,… searching for the word of the Lord, but they will not find it" (Am 8:12).

Bible scholars have suggested that Jesus sin-convicted the accusers of the adulteress by silently writing their sins in the dust (see John 8:6-8). God doesn't pout and he doesn't shout, but he does clearly convey his displeasure to those who disregard his promptings of grace. His "silence of disapproval" is gently corrective and effective.

If the Lord's "silence of disapproval" (not condemnation) seems to turn your prayers into monologues rather than dialogues, perhaps you are not fully responding to his gentle grace-nudges. Doesn't his silence mercifully enable you to hear your conscience?

God's Silence of Love

In the British navy, when an explosion or any sudden disaster occurs, the bugler's duty is to play immediately what is called "The Still." It is a signal for each person to remain perfectly quiet for a moment to calm himself to prepare for panic-free and well thought-out action in the emergency.

The trumpet clarion call of the prophet (see Psalms 46:10), "Be still and know that I am God!," is a kind of bugle signal for us to stop in our tracks and acknowledge God in our life. His own silence can make us aware of our noisy freneticism. The prophet Zephaniah tells us (3:17) that the Lord "will quiet you with his love." But perhaps equally significant is an alternate translation: "He will be quiet in his love."

Just as we can experience a deep and loving sympathy while wordlessly embracing a bereaved person, by that same silent act we can quiet the anguish in the heart of that same person. Thus, the love within our own heart can be silent, but it can also silence the hurt of another in some way. That same twofold characteristic can be found in God's silent love. If we are sensitive enough to detect the waves of his silent love washing over us, our own heart becomes silent and we can then really "know that he is God" in all the profound meaning that those words entail. In this way, his silent love is not seen as divine aloofness but as sacred intimacy, which will launch our prayer life into mystical depths.

44

Ever think about "getting away from it all"? You might want to reconsider. Scientists discovered that laboratory rats exposed to only *one week* of conditions simulating modern city life—flashing lights, loud noise, crowding, and so on—demonstrate signs of irritability, aggressiveness, and *permanent* hypertension (high blood pressure). Imagine what these conditions do to humans over the course of time!

External stress from noise pollution by radio, TV, street sounds, sirens, nearby conversations, etc. is coupled with internal stress of worry, fear, distractions, deadline pressures, etc. to make our lives seem like a pressure-cooker existence. We get so accustomed to such pressures that for some, "structured quietude" can cause boredom and even anxiety. Yet, like water in a clear spring, or pure fresh mountain air, a program of regular exterior and interior quiet can be spiritually refreshing as well as therapeutic. That is why all religious traditions emphasize the need of at least periodic withdrawal from life's frenetic pace.

Two suggestions: Make *full* use of the naturally occurring moments of silence that lend themselves to serene meditation; and second, set aside a period of fifteen minutes or a half-hour each day to commune with God. (Read Matthew 6:6.) I know a woman who sets her alarm a half hour earlier for this purpose; and an office worker who takes a daily "prayer break" with his lunch break at a nearby park. Read how Jesus did it (see Luke 5:15-16; 6:12). You can too.

Quiet, you'll like it!

45

When violin strings were made of catgut and the bows were strung with horsehair, one unimaginative boor described violin-playing as "drawing the tail of a horse over the guts of a cat." That's enough to de-romanticize any tableside violin serenade!

Merely surface-viewing life's events depletes them of all fascination and makes life itself almost meaningless. The sport of golf would be simply hitting a ball and chasing it to hit it again until it goes in a hole! Ballet would be just jumping up and down. Sculpture would be simply chipping pieces from a block of stone.

Perceiving a wider dimension of one's existence is a sign of human maturity, beyond an infant's way of viewing things. A worried, self-preoccupied man walking through a forest doesn't really see the beauty of the trees or the marvels of nature. His narrow mental vision anesthetizes his real awareness of his environment and the sense of mystery. Looking beyond the symbol into that which is symbolized is the rationale for religious vestments, or sacramentals like ashes on Ash Wednesday, incense, and oil. Only by a deeper look can one appreciate human dignity and rights in self and others. It is a skill that requires practice.

Start practicing, for instance, by looking below the surface of hard-to-love persons and seeing the hidden Jesus-presence there. "Whatever you did for one of the least of these brothers of mine, you did for me" (Mt 25:40).

Listen Up!

46 Much of our astronomical knowledge today comes from listening rather than looking. The listeners are "radio astronomers" whose enormous antennas constantly scan the skies for squawks, beeps, and hums that reveal far more about the universe than the eye can see. It may even be the only way of detecting possible life in space.

"Listening with the heart" may be the only way we will ever detect the most subtle needs of humans all around us—far more than can be seen by the eye. When people speak to us we usually pay attention only to the obvious meaning of their words, but neglect to hear a deeper underlying message, not fully articulated. Only by listening with our heart can we meet them in their suffering, reach out with empathy to heal their hurts, budge the vast distance of their emotional and spiritual isolation.

By listening to the below-the-surface messages of hurting persons, we acquire a side effect of becoming more aware of our own prejudices, selfishness, and lack of concern for others. A truly good listener begins to have the attitude of Christ (see Philippians 2:5), who enables comfort to flow through us (see 2 Corinthians 1:5) as we perceive persons' needs the way God does. We thus learn to respond with his love and pity: "I have indeed seen the misery of my people.... I have heard them crying out.... I am concerned about their suffering. So I have come down to rescue them" (Ex 3:7-8).

Touchstone of Love

An opal is one of the less lustrous gems to be found in any jewelry store. But it is called the "sympathetic jewel" because it bursts into colorful iridescence when it is warmed by human touch.

Persons, too, are "warmed" by human touch. The earliest stage of love is the tactile stage, when our love development is set into motion the first moment we feel our mother's gentle caress. Through the skin, with its millions of small receptors, we most directly contact the world around us. It is the organ by which we first experience care and tenderness.

Throughout life this sense of touch remains important in human—and even animal—relationships. When physical touch is not appropriate, one can touch the hearts of others with exquisite sensitivity. Sensitive persons are always aware of how brusque words, actions, or even tone of voice may hurt others, and how respect and gentleness can support and encourage and heal.

Think for a moment of those you encounter at home or at work or elsewhere. How have you been "in touch" with them—by kindly gesture, compliment, encouragement, or gift of time? Resolve to "reach out and touch" them. Envelop them with a touch of *expressed* love, as the situation allows. As Shakespeare wrote in *Two Gentlemen of Verona,* "They do not love that do not show their love."

Open Mouth, Insert Foot

48   "Foot-in-mouth" disease is common in these days of political sensitivity. The poor become "economically marginalized," a retarded person "cerebrally challenged," while the elderly are "chronologically gifted."

Jesus was far more straightforward and uncluttered in his speech, and urged us to speak likewise: "Simply let your 'Yes' be 'Yes,' and your 'No,' 'No'; anything beyond this comes from the evil one" (Mt 5:37). Having just decried the need for oaths, Jesus implied that oath-taking presupposes a sinful weakness of the human race, namely a tendency to lie that "comes from the evil one"—the father of lies. If no one ever lied, there would be no need for oaths to affirm the truth, and a simple "yes" or "no" would be accepted as a truth-revealing response.

Language, technology, and even crime grow more complex daily. Christianity must counterpoint this tangled complexity with holy pristine simplicity. As "sheep among wolves," we must be "in the world but not of it," while coping with its evil intrigue—being "shrewd as snakes and as *innocent* as doves" (Mt 10:16) Paul invites us to try childlike (not childish) simplicity: "In regard to evil be infants, but in your thinking be adults" (1 Cor 14:20).

God's Pretty Smart

"God's pretty smart," observed a perspicacious fourth-grader. "Long before eyeglasses were invented, he put our nose and ears in the right places."

Job, too, saw something of God's loving providence in the shaping of the human body. "Your hands shaped me and made me," he mused. "Did you not... clothe me with skin and flesh and knit me together with bones and sinews? You gave me life and showed me kindness, and in your providence watched over my spirit" (Jb 10:8-12).

Unless we pause, like these two did, to think about such marvels, we tend to take for granted God's providence in our lives—even in our very bodies and their awesome functions. A man healed of blindness is grateful beyond compare for the gift of his restored eyesight, while the sighted person seldom, if ever, exults in God's gift of eyesight.

Pause now, and think of the providential design of your heart that beats without your conscious effort, your skin with its built-in thermostat, your hearing that transforms air vibrations into meaningful sound in communication and music appreciation, your digestion that extracts and distributes nourishment from food. Then let your heart exult, "How great thou art, O Lord!"

Body Language Spoken Here

50 In times of persecution, early Christians needed some swift inconspicuous gesture to identify themselves to one another. Since a Christian is one who follows Christ, the challenge of Christ himself suggested the gesture to be used: "If anyone would come after me, he must... *take up his cross* and follow me" (Mk 8:34). Thus the sign of the cross, a secret gesture at first, later became an open public act of professing the Christian faith.

Body language bespeaks externally what is present internally. Religious gestures in body language (kneeling, standing up, genuflecting, praying with hands folded or uplifted, or striking one's breast) express various attitudes of relating to God. But body language in the sign of the cross externally expresses (professes) *multiple* facts of Christian belief: belief in Jesus' death on the cross, by which we were redeemed (see Colossians 2:13), by which the Mosaic law was canceled (v. 14), and by which Jesus crushed the powers of hell (v. 15). It expresses belief in the Incarnation—for only as a human could God die on the cross (see Hebrews 2:14); and belief in the Trinity, invoked verbally with the action. It depicts our intent to enter into Jesus' paschal mystery by dying to self with him and rising to a new life with him (see Romans 8:11; 11:15; Ephesians 2:5).

These basic Christian (not just Catholic) beliefs expressed by the sign of the cross make it a most sublime form of body language, a sign of the times, for all times—and all Christians.

Why Can't You Tickle Yourself?

This is a question with a good news/bad news kind of answer. The bad news is that no one really knows the answer; it's one of countless mysteries still unsolved by science. The good news is that all mysteries, both scientific and religious, will be known eventually—most of them probably in the next life.

This is true of the weightier issues, such as the reality of suffering, as well as the less "ticklish" mysteries. It was the mystery of suffering that bothered the psalmist: "All day long I have been plagued; I have been punished.... When I tried to understand all this, it was oppressive to me till I entered the sanctuary of God; then I understood" (Ps 73:14, 16-17). Job was given a similar mystical insight after complaining about the mystery of suffering: "I spoke of things I did not understand,... but now my eyes have seen you... I despise myself and repent" (Jb 42:3, 5-6).

Paul had to confess that God's ways are inscrutable (Rom 11:33). What Paul calls "God's secret wisdom, a wisdom that has been hidden" (1 Cor 2:7) can be frustrating to the ever-curious human mind; not even all natural scientific mysteries can be solved, much less the supernatural ones. Perhaps this is God's clever way of making us humble. By realizing that we lack the omniscience of God, we are humbled into submitting to him in reverence and awe.

52

Garbage collectors are somewhat taken for granted as they go about their malodorous task. But their importance becomes obvious when a city-wide garbage collectors' strike erupts; that's when the maggoty garbage piles up day after day, as flies and rats breed freely. If the strike is unresolved, the threat of disease sets in. In some ways our health depends on garbage collectors as much as it does on doctors and other caregivers.

It is Jesus, our spiritual "garbage collector," who removes our sinful soul-garbage that spreads through every part of us, contaminating the heart, mind, imagination, memory, and especially the soul itself.

Everyone needs garbage removed. As Romans tells us: "All have sinned and fall short of the glory of God" (Rom 3:23). Yet, for garbage to be collected, two things must be done: First, we must put the garbage out, as David did: "I acknowledged my sin to you.... I will confess my transgressions to the Lord" (Ps 32:5). Secondly, we must let the Lord do the work: "and *you* forgave the guilt of my sin." It is not we who overcome sin with Jesus' help, but Jesus with our help (that is, our repentance).

But we can do even more—we can stay garbage-free thereafter. How? By simply living in him in loving intimacy, says John: "No one who lives in him keeps on sinning" (1 Jn 3:6). A truly God-centered person may not be totally free of faults, but such a person's life is not characterized by sinfulness.

The "Laurel and Hardy" Principle

Stan Laurel and Oliver Hardy, the comedy team whose names are almost a household doublet, made 105 movies together. But few of their nostalgic fans ever heard of the 76 movies that Laurel made without Hardy, or the 213 movies that Hardy made without Laurel.

Like ham and eggs, fish and chips, lox and bagels, or corned beef and cabbage, some things seem to be meant to go together. And that is true for persons as well—like a happily married couple, or close friends, or compatible business partners (see Ecclesiastes 4:9-12). And often it's not just two persons in conjunction, but also large or small groups accomplishing things cooperatively that couldn't be done alone, whether it be space launches, Rose Bowl parades, or prayer groups. As Aristotle said, humans are social animals and hence interdependent. Philosophically, this principle finds its spiritual validation in the Bible's command for church attendance (see Hebrews 10:25) and its endorsement of family devotions (see Acts 10:2).

This same grouping principle was sublimated by Jesus' promise that even the smallest Christ-centered group could draw down from heaven answers to prayer, and also the personal presence of Jesus himself: "I tell you that if two of you on earth agree about anything you ask for, it will be done for you by my Father in heaven. For where two or three come together *in my name*, there am I with them" (Mt 18:19-20). Some graces are found only in groups where Jesus is present; don't miss becoming empowered and God-hugged!

54   The Mayan Indians admired the looks of slightly cross-eyed people. To cause it in their own children, they hung beads close to their babies' faces. Deliberate and often grotesque deforming of the body has been common in many aboriginal tribes—and it is not altogether uncommon in the more "civilized" segments of some societies (including ours): tattooing, nose- and tongue-piercing, knife-scarring of skin, neck-stretching, foot-binding, and navel ring wearing.

Appropriate haircutting, nail-trimming, or use of cosmetics to make the body socially more presentable is not necessarily bad, *if* it is not outright vanity. But to impair physical function or to unnecessarily mutilate the body shows a basic lack of appreciation of one's own human dignity. Like the human soul, the body has its own intrinsic dignity and nobility, as we know from biblical revelation: first, as it relates to Christian eschatology: "God raised the Lord from the dead, and he will raise us also. Do you not know that your bodies are members of Christ himself?" (1 Cor 6:14-15). (This, by the way, is the basis for the devotional use of bodily relics of the saints.)

Secondly, Paul extols our bodily dignity in the context of chastity: "He who sins sexually sins against his own body. Do you not know that your body is a temple of the Holy Spirit?... Therefore honor God with your body" (vv. 18-20). What a privilege—to think that we can honor God with our bodies, not just our souls!

Default of De Conscience

A conscience-smitten tax cheat sent $500 to the IRS, adding that he hadn't slept well since he defaulted on his taxes in 1980. "If I don't sleep better now," he added, "I'll send the rest."

"Sleeping with a good conscience" can be said to be one of the rewards of practicing real honesty, but it's certainly not the only one. God has his own gracious ways of rewarding honesty, even in this life. That's why Paul sought to be honest both in the eyes of men and in the eyes of God (see 2 Corinthians 8:21).

Shakespeare wrote, "Take note, O world! To be direct and honest is not safe." Honesty carries a certain "risk"—the risk of losing opportunities for illicit gain. As true Christians, our honesty should be above "risk"—practiced solely to please God.

After repenting of his "dishonesty" in committing adultery and conspiracy to murder, David experienced God's rewarding love: "The Lord has rewarded me according to my righteousness, according to my cleanness in his sight" (2 Sm 22:25). What, precisely, was David's earthly reward for honesty? It was the same as that promised to all honest persons, as the first psalm tells us: delight in God's word, spiritual fruitfulness, success in human endeavors, and divine protection. Jesus said "those with a noble and good heart" will hear his word and retain it, and by persevering will produce a bounteous crop (see Luke 8:15). *Of course* it pays to be honest!

56

The statistics are impressive. One hour of moderate physical exercise will extend the life span of the average person by two hours. Mental exercise is also known to substantially lower the risk of senility in old age; one's mind could be kept sharp well into the senior years by a crossword puzzle hobby or by challenging one's mind in intellectual study.

So much for the exercise of body and mind. But what about exercising the spirit? Paul speaks of the need for wholeness in all three (see 1 Thessalonians 5:23). Without statistics, but with divine inspiration, he assigns to spiritual exercise a clear priority: "Physical training is of some value," he writes, "but godliness has value for all things, holding promise for both the present life and the life to come" (1 Tm 4:8). Unlike physical conditioning, offering its "two-hour gain for one-hour pain," "godliness with contentment is *great* gain" (6:6). One hour of exercising our spirit will reap inestimable rewards in time and in eternity, he says. One hour of fervent prayer, for example, or one hour of humble and love-charged service to another human, or one hour of loving resignation to God's will in the midst of harrowing anguish will reap certainly more than two hours of heavenly bliss.

"Let us throw off... the sin that so easily entangles, and let us run with perseverance the race marked out for us" (Heb 12:1): The prize? We're not talking hours here—we're talking eternity!

Now Ear This!

After a street fight, a Chicago man found himself in the awkward situation of having one ear on his head and another on his stomach. The ear on his stomach had been detached in the fight, and was surgically implanted in his abdomen between layers of skin and muscle to heal there before being reattached to his head. His hospital visitors clowned with him by talking to his tummy.

If we would "have the ear" of someone with whom we want to communicate, we need to "have an ear for" what they want to say to us. People are more disposed to listen to us if we listen to them. And so is God. When God's people "stopped their ears" to his word, in his anger he told Zechariah, "When I called, they did not listen; so when they called, I would not listen" (Zec 7:13). God has warned those who turn a deaf ear to his will for them, "Although they shout in my ears, I will not listen to them" (Ez 8:18). The Lord will "bend an ear" to us only if we habitually "lend an ear" to him.

Of course, he really wants to hear from us, by way of praise and petition; but he wants even more for us to hear from him. Yet, as Shakespeare wrote in *Hamlet*, "Ears are senseless that should give us hearing." Listen! God is speaking now—in his word, by his inspirations of grace, and by the promptings of our conscience.

Light at the End of Our Troubles?

58

Before you finish reading this sentence, someone will be dead of starvation who was alive when you started it. This very minute thirty people will die of starvation. That's one death every two seconds—not from all causes, but one alone: food deprivation!

The World Health Organization estimates that one-third of the world is well-fed, one-third is underfed, and the other third is starving. Seventy percent of the world's children under the age of six are undernourished; due to lack of food, 200 million of them are affected by mental retardation or blindness, and another 10 million are hunger-diseased.

This unthinkable suffering, due primarily to poverty, waste, theft, war, greed, and poor distribution techniques, provides an excuse for atheists and agnostics to conclude that human existence in general is one big morass of meaningless suffering and death. That would be true, of course, if there were no afterlife.

To counterpoint this nihilistic mentality, one theologian listed fifty-six biblically stated reasons for suffering as part of God's permissive will. Consider just one of those reasons. Take a closer look at your own suffering and ponder Paul's words from 2 Corinthians 4:16-17: "We do not lose heart.... Outwardly we are wasting away, yet inwardly we are being renewed day by day. For our light and momentary troubles are achieving for us an eternal glory that far outweighs them all."

Under Niagara's Waters

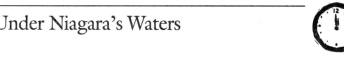

On the American side of Niagara Falls, the colossal sheet of water takes a dizzying leap over a precipice to crash 160 feet below. But between the face of that precipice and the great overleaping rush of water is the vacant space called the Cave of the Winds, where guides lead rain-geared tourists into a thunderous, awesome envelope of splashing spray and mist, what appears to be hardly an arm's length from the crushing downpour of water.

The excitement from the crashing noise and water's rush is not enough to overshadow one's sense of security in knowing that the waterflow will maintain its swiftness so as not to narrow its overarching distance from the observation platform.

It is possible to experience God's peace flowing "like a river" (Is 48:18), even in the noisome and unsettling times in which we live, but only for those who truly trust in the Lord. His ever-flowing love provides protection and security—and consequent peace—even as endless dangers and threats rush close by us constantly. Deep inner peace is available to anyone who has mastered the art of *trusting* in his love; the classic words of Isaiah 26:3 frame this truth with trenchant poignancy: "You will keep in perfect peace him whose mind is steadfast, *because he trusts in you.*"

Life is an exciting Niagara adventure. When we trust in God's ever-flowing love, he drenches us with his peace and security.

How Does Your Garden Grow?

60

An executive officer at Standard Oil Company, during his daily Bible reading, was struck by the passage of Exodus 2:3, where it states that the baby Moses was set afloat in the Nile in a papyrus basket waterproofed with tar and pitch. The officer knew that where tar or pitch oozed from the ground there must be oil. So he sent a geologist to explore the area, and the resultant oil discovery enabled Egypt to become a major oil-producing nation.

The Bible reveals, both explicitly and implicitly, boundless information about material things, from oil deposit locations to hygiene principles and nutrition. But more importantly, it reveals *spiritual* information, along with inspiration and encouragement. This deep soul-enrichment is enjoyed by devout souls. But why do some respond only momentarily to Scripture reading? And why are others turned off by it altogether?

The answer lies in the parable of the sower, with the four kinds of "soil" in which God's word is sown (see Matthew 13, Mark 4; Luke 8). First, there is the hard-packed footpath where unrooted seed is snatched away by the devil; this speaks of a heart hardened by pride or other sin. The second type of soil, sub-layered with shale rock causing the shallow-rooted word to wither, is like the heart that is looking for a subjective, "feel-good" religion with no strings attached. The third type of soil, the soil overgrown with nettles, is like the soul choked with pleasures and money worries. It is only the fourth type of soil—the truly good, fertile soil—that produces soul-enriching fruit.

Answer the question honestly: Which type are you?

Some Plead Ignorance,
Others Breed Ignorance

When questioned by his Sunday school teacher as to who defeated the Philistines, the lad's disinterested response was, "I dunno. I don't follow the minor leagues."

Ignorance comes in two models: culpable and inculpable. The former implies malice in refusing to learn what God wants us to know. The latter is not malicious. Peter—echoing Jesus' words, "They know not what they do"—excused the Jews for disowning Christ: "You acted in ignorance, as did your leaders" (Acts 3:17). Conscience can thus be either well-formed or malformed (ignorant), sometimes accusing, sometimes excusing (see Romans 2:15).

God's wrath falls on any who *refuse* to properly form their conscience, who "by their wickedness suppress the truth" (Rom 1:18 RSV). "Although they know God, they neither glorify him nor thank him... their thinking is futile... and their hearts are darkened" (1:21). But God's loving mercy is bestowed on sincere truth-seekers like Paul: "I was shown mercy because I acted in ignorance" (1 Tm 1:13).

We all suffer from spiritual ignorance in many ways. There is much more we need to learn about God's love for us in Christ. Let us ask for grace "to grasp how wide and long and high and deep is the love of Christ, and to *know* this love that surpasses knowledge" and be filled with "the fullness of God" (Eph 3:18-19).

Nothing Left but God

62 On his last day at work before a layoff, a Los Angeles man received an emergency call to hurry home, where he was horrified to find his house in ashes and his wife and four small children dead. Totally bereft of family, house, job, and even insurance, he wept in his neighbor's arms, "I have nothing left now but God."

No one can pass through life without experiencing some loss. It may be abandonment, divorce, financial loss, job loss, loss of a friend, or loss of our good reputation. For some people, like starving war refugees or those tortured or imprisoned injustly, the deprivations reach the very limits of human endurance. The sign of a truly authentic Christian is the ability to submit every aspect of life to the lordship of Christ. We learn to trust in God's permissive will, which sometimes includes physical evils such as pain and poverty. In so doing, we know that some good will eventuate from these things: "We know that in everything God works for good with those who love him, who are called according to his purpose" (Rm 8:28, RSV).

When we endure hardship, we should try to echo King David's words of hope: "My Lord, apart from you I have no good thing" (Ps 16:2).

Odd Man Out

Pythagoras, the Greek philosopher, regarded even numbers as feminine and odd numbers as masculine. He preferred odd numbers, freely admitting his prejudice against the even, "feminine" ones. This is one mild example of how women have been treated as second-class citizens for centuries. And it is no wonder that many women today have protested this treatment—in some circles quite militantly!

Of course, Jesus was the first real champion of righteous and rightful feminism. How he loved and cherished those women (there were "many" of them, writes Matthew), his fellow travelers from Galilee to Jerusalem, supporting him financially and taking care of him (see Matthew 27:55; Luke 8:2-3). They were the *first* to hear the angel's news report describing the resurrection, the *first* to see Jesus in his glorified body, and the *first* ones assigned by him to evangelize even his apostles, by announcing the Resurrection (see Matthew 28:5-10).

With such noble and God-recognized prestige, no wonder the first pope, Peter, wrote that husbands should respect and *honor* their wives, if they want their prayers answered! (see 1 Peter 3:7). That "honor-women-or-else" warning, if heeded by all, could change the very fiber of modern family life, and hence all of society!

A Tree in Every Acorn

64

There was a favorite portage spot on Lake Michigan where traders hauled their canoes ashore to lug them to the rivers that linked with the Mississippi. That portage spot grew to become Chicago.

What may seem most insignificant to us may be of colossal value in God's eyes, "'for my thoughts are not your thoughts'... says the Lord. 'As high as the heavens are above the earth... so high are... my thoughts above your thoughts'" (Is 55:8-9, NAB). Knowing the exact number of hairs on your head seems trivial, but God has them all numbered (see Matthew 10:30; Luke 12:7). And giving a cup of water is almost nothing, but anyone doing so in the name of Jesus "will certainly not lose his reward" (Mt 10:42; Mk 9:41).

What makes small things look so big in God's "magnifying glass"? It's the presence of our Christ-focused love. Feeding the hungry or giving drink to the thirsty, or doing even the *tiniest* love-filled act to even "the *least* of these my brethren," (Mt 25:40, RSV) is really done for Jesus. The *big* deal is the final payoff: "Come, take your inheritance, the kingdom prepared for you."

The Computer between Your Ears

The most complex object in the known material universe is the human brain. No other physical entity even knows there *is* a universe. Cats, cows, and cockroaches don't know there's a universe or that it has a Creator. Neither do crocuses, carrots, or cacti. More obviously, neither do crystals, chrome, or cryolite. Only an intellect—which in living humans is instrumented by the brain—can consciously appreciate the ingenious Creator of the universe.

Conscious, deliberate honoring of the Creator constitutes "formal" praise. But *every* creature by its very existence gives "material" praise (see Psalm 148)—reflecting God's own "be-ing." Christians give *material* praise—"that we... might *be* for the praise of his glory" (Eph. 1:12)—but we also give *formal* praise by declaring his praises (see 1 Peter 2:9). Persons who seldom or never *formally* praise God fail in their ultimate human destiny.

The third way we bring honor to our Creator is by imitating his holiness to the best of our ability. Renew your resolve to become and stay holy, for "the fruit of righteousness... [is] the praise of God" (Phil 1:11).

66

About twenty percent of a ladder's cost covers the manufacturer's liability insurance on that ladder. We live in a dangerous world—and in a litigious society, for which *everyone* pays. There are physical risks for the buyer and financial risks for the seller. Even with all the breaks, life is a walk on very thin ice.

But a soul risk beats a body risk, hands down. Who says? Jesus says—in the form of a simple but profound question: "What can a man give in exchange for his soul?" (Mt 16:26; see Mark 8:36; Luke 9:25). There's no risk in striving to save your soul, but there's great risk in *not* striving to do so. Repeatedly Jesus compares the risks of earthly vs. eternal life: "Whoever wants to save his life will lose it, but whoever loses his life for me will find it" (Mt 16:25; see Matthew 10:39; Mark 8:35; Luke 9:24, 17:33).

You will probably never experience risks like those of Paul and Barnabas—men who risked their lives for the name of Jesus (see Acts 15:26). But you may have to risk ridicule from fellow workers for Bible reading during your lunch break, or a scolding from an uncompassionate confessor, or a spouse's complaint for watching religious TV, or a teenager's rebellion against family prayer. Stand firm with Paul: "Who shall separate us from the love of Christ?... Trouble or hardship or persecution... or danger or sword?" (Rom 8:35). It's worth the risk!

What a Waste!

On the average, one out of every 466 photos taken by *National Geographic* photographers ends up in print. The overwhelming odds are that even potentially prize-winning photos will be file-buried. What a waste of talent, time, effort, and money!

Our western society is disgraced by its disregard of simple thrift. Consider the cavalier waste of food in restaurants and cruise ships in light of the fact that over forty thousand people die of starvation worldwide every day! Not to mention other kinds of widespread waste of talent, skills, time, effort, and money.

But far more tragic than all these forms of waste is the incalculable waste of suffering. How is suffering wasted? In numerous ways: by resentment against God for sending or permitting it; by not undergoing it with holy abandonment to God's will; by self-pity; by complaining petulantly; by not offering it as a sacrifice to the glory of God; by not using it as an occasion of developing patience, fortitude, character, and even hope (see Romans 5:3-4), and above all, by not *rejoicing* "that you participate in the sufferings of Christ, so that you may be overjoyed when his glory is revealed" (1 Pt 4:13). Every pain or tribulation is a "coupon" redeemable for a heavenly fortune. Don't waste it!

68

Phobias and panic attacks are being treated success-fully with only seven weekly sessions by the use of virtual reality therapy at Georgia Tech. The new technology projects a phobic situation of apparent reality, helping the patient to be reconditioned gradually to a normal response to heights, flying, tunnels, and dogs. Even one session of "VR" can convince the mind to readily accept as real something that is not.

Life is full of reality counterfeits. Many persons judged by the courts as guilty are really innocent, and vice versa. Many actions of others that seem malicious are not, and many malicious acts can be made to look innocent—as every con man soon learns. But God sees ultimate reality: "Man looks at the outward appearance, but the Lord looks at the heart" (1 Sm 16:7). "The Lord searches every heart and understands every *motive* behind the *thoughts*" (1 Chr 28:9). One's motives are fomented in the will (or "heart") and one's conscious thoughts reside in the mind. These two faculties provide the subjective norms of all morality. In good acts, these two conform to the objective norm (God's law).

God's words can be either uplifting or sobering: "I the Lord search the *heart* and examine the *mind*, to reward a man according to his conduct, according to what his deeds deserve" (Jer 17:10). The sincere person welcomes the "righteous God, who searches *minds* and *hearts*" (Ps 7:9), but the sinner might well quail before him.

A Saint I Ain't

You've heard about the crook who made counterfeit pennies. He was caught because he put the heads and tails on the wrong sides.

We often don't know which side is which; sinners are often saintly and saints are often "sinnerly." Yet "*all* have sinned and fall short of the glory of God" (Rom 3:23). From the cradle we're known as sinners, but from the casket we may seem like saints.

But if you think saints are hard to find today, just try to find someone who acknowledges himself as a sinner! Acknowledged *sinners* are an endangered species—perhaps because so few *sins* are any longer acknowledged. Yet sin by any other name is still sin in God's eyes. "He who conceals his sins does not prosper, but whoever confesses and renounces them finds mercy" (Prv 28:13).

Suppose the Prodigal Son, on his return, had said, "Well, you know how it is, Dad. Everyone has a fling once in a while." Without anesthetizing his guilt, he simply said remorsefully, "Father, I have sinned" (Lk 15:21).

How refreshingly honest—and cleansing! "If we confess our sins, he… will purify us from all unrighteousness" (1 Jn 1:9).

70

A nun asked her fourth graders to write a story of how they would spend their time with Jesus if he were to visit them for a day. After a pause, one lad asked, "How do you spell 'Toys-R-Us'?"

Jesus, whose appellation was "Emmanuel," meaning "God with us," promised to be with us not just for a day, but "to the very end of the age" (Mt 28:20). The "practice of the presence of God," even wordlessly, is quintessential prayer, and has four forms, says St. Alphonsus.

First, we can vividly imagine the real but spiritual presence of Jesus as our constant companion. (Do not confuse this with his real *physical* sacramental presence *within* us in Holy Communion or that presence *with* us when visiting the Blessed Sacrament.)

Second, we can, by fervent faith, be aware of being totally encompassed by the Lord who observes our every thought, word, and action, *as if* we were the only creature he was aware of, as he plans an incalculable reward for each virtuous activity of ours.

Third, awareness of his presence can be found in creatures, especially other humans, as reflections of his divine goodness.

Fourth, by love: "If anyone loves me,... my Father will love him, and we will come... and make our home with him" (Jn 14:23).

Could'a, Would'a, Should'a

In two lines, John Greenleaf Whittier formulated a kind of success vs. failure philosophy of life in his classic distich:

> For all sad words of tongue or pen,
> The saddest are these: "It might have been!"

Thoughts of regret, either casual or overwhelming, arise from rearview mirror glances at our various "could'a, would'a, should'a" situations. These can range from a cavalier "too bad I messed up" reaction to a deeply remorseful sense of loss. It may be a simple wrong turn while driving, or a neglect of a now-expired store sale or appliance warranty, or neglecting to buy into a soaring stock market option. More serious regrets might include an avoidable car accident, perhaps fatal to another, or finding oneself terminally ill with lung cancer or emphysema from years of smoking. Regretful situations are endless.

"It might have been!" That thought is the greatest torment of reprobate souls in hell, who are now painfully aware of the fact that they are forever deprived of heaven's rapturous bliss because they freely chose to remain distanced from God by their unrepented sin. This ultimate regret, the eternal "might have been" remorse, was poignantly expressed by Jesus: "For what will it profit a man, if he gains the whole world and forfeits his life?" (Mt 16:26, RSV).

72

Just as a human being may die of extreme sleep deprivation—a death preceded by total disorientation (insanity)—an immortal soul can "die" when it is deprived of grace (by the committing of mortal sin). "There is a sin that leads to death," John reminds us (see 1 John 5:16).

This kind of spiritual death is also preceded by a kind of "spiritual insanity," of which there are two primary forms. The first type is a deadening of the conscience, an outrageous disregard of the heinousness of seriously offending the infinite majesty of God. The second is a total disregard of the unspeakable suffering from eternal hellfire that awaits the unrepentant sinner. Each of these two forms of spiritual insanity has a cure, and applied cures will revive the "dying" soul, restoring the life of grace.

The first cure is a "godly sorrow" that "brings repentance" (2 Cor 7:10). This kind of remorse is based on love for God whom one has offended, and is called perfect contrition. The second antidote (imperfect contrition) is a remorse for sin because of fear of punishment: "The wicked will not go unpunished" (Prv 11:21). This fear refers not just to any sanction (such as the embarrassment of appearing foolish), but God-assigned punishment. (This makes it *supernatural* contrition, even though "imperfect.")

To assure that any act of contrition is authentic, one needs a "firm purpose of amendment"—*intending* to avoid sin and the near "occasions" of sin. This releases God's life-giving forgiveness.

Furor over a Juror

When John Lambert was called for jury duty in a drug trial in New York, he was willing to serve, but was disqualified because it was discovered that he happened to be the defendant in that case. "I was prepared to find myself not guilty," he protested.

If we were allowed to determine the outcome of our own trial at the final judgment, could we be as objective as God, who "will judge the world in righteousness and... truth" (Ps 96:13)? If we deliberately continue in sin, we might well have a fearful expectation of judgment and of raging fire. But if we repent of our sin with heartfelt contrition, the judgment will be in our favor, for God's mercy would exculpate us. Remember, our attorney is the very best—"one who speaks to the Father in our defense—Jesus Christ, the Righteous One" (see 1 John 2:1).

In a civil court, remorse for a crime doesn't usually exempt the criminal from the sentencing. But in God's court, "*godly* sorrow brings repentance that leads to salvation" (2 Cor 7:10). Why? Because of the love behind God's fathomless mercy, which tempers his justice. "Because of his great *love* for us, God, who is rich in mercy, made us alive with Christ even when we were dead in transgressions—it is by grace you have been saved" (Eph 2:4).

Washing Instructions

74   Older readers may remember "Bathless Groggins" as the scurfy, fly-blown character in the old-time *Li'l Abner* cartoon strip, who prided himself on his never having bathed. If he served no other purpose, grubby old "Bathless" led me to thank God that I would never be forced to live a lifetime totally unwashed.

Just as the body needs cleansing, so also the soul. "Having our bodies washed," we need also to "draw near to God,... having our hearts sprinkled to cleanse us from a guilty conscience" (Heb 10:22). The psalmist struggled to keep his heart cleansed: "In vain have I kept my heart pure; in vain have I washed my hands in innocence" (Ps 73:13). But our God likes to bathe his sin-splattered children every time they need it.

I've always felt that the motto, "cleanliness is next to godliness," should read, "cleanliness *is* godliness"—when it refers to cleanliness of soul, by which it resembles the purity of God himself. As Paul tells the repentant Corinthians, "You were washed, you were *sanctified*" (1 Cor 6:11). This sanctifying "washing" leads us to a saving "washing": "He *saved* us through the washing of rebirth and renewal by the Holy Spirit, whom he poured out on us generously" (Ti 3:5-6).

If you enjoy a bath, that's the ultimate bathing experience!

Complete Delete

The average adult today can remember the time when computers were unheard of, or at least not regarded as a home appliance. Yet today, if all computers stopped working, our highly technological society would be rendered helpless and the economy would collapse.

The primary advantage of cybernetics is perhaps the ability to store and retrieve virtually limitless information. But this boon would become a burden if unwanted items could not be deleted. As a safety feature some computers ask, "Are you sure you want this deleted?" With a tap of a single key, the data is deleted forever.

The Lord has, in his own divine "technology," a "deleting" function, erasing our sins as irretrievably as a computer erases a file. "I am he who *blots out* your transgressions... and *remembers your sins no more*" (Is 43:25). But he first asks us if we are *sure* we want our sins erased, because he's familiar with the "false repentance" of those who seek God's forgiveness without taking steps to avoid future sin. In asking us, "Are you sure?" he's really asking "Are you sincere?" If our answer is affirmative, the key we then push to delete the sin is repentance: "Repent... and turn to God, so that your sins may be *wiped out*" (Acts 3:19).

A computer with no delete button would be an inconvenience. But God without a "delete function"... the thought is terrifying!

76

A rooster has a crest of head feathers. They flatten when he loses a cockfight. That's the origin of the word, "crestfallen."

To be "crestfallen" is to be disconsolate or discouraged; and this state of mind can even devolve into a dark form of despair, while the depressed person is not even aware of the reason for it. The psalmist in a triple refrain asked the question: "Why are you downcast, O my soul? Why so disturbed within me?" He then proposes to himself the antidote: "Put your hope in God, for I will yet praise him, my Savior and my God" (Ps 42:5, 11; see Psalms 43:5).

By putting his hope in his "Savior and God," David implicitly referred to the role of the expected Messiah as a depression healer, for a major part of the messianic mission of Jesus was "to bind up the brokenhearted" (Is 61:1) and "to release the oppressed" (Lk 4:18).

From a mild case of the "Monday morning blues" to the serious state of suicidal depression requiring psychotherapy, there is always available for the "crestfallen" the loving support of the depressed Man of Sorrows, who in the Garden of Gethsemane was "overwhelmed with sorrow to the point of death" (Mt 26:38). Yet, paradoxically, it is that same "Man of Sorrows, familiar with suffering" (Is 53:3), who lovingly prescribes an antidepressant: "my joy… in you, that your joy may be complete" (Jn 15:11).

Where Is the Goalpost?

It may sound simplistic, but the very first thing one must learn in order to play football successfully is to learn where the goalpost is—the *right* goalpost, that is! How often has a touchdown been scored for the opposing team when a dazed player ran with the ball in the wrong direction, to the cheers of the opposition!

If we lose sight of our proper goal in life, we may find ourselves gratifying the Enemy and his cheering section in Hades. It's alarmingly easy to become confused about our real goal, if we submit to the subtle allurements of the world. "Everything in the world—the cravings of sinful man, the lust of his eyes and the boasting of what he has and does—comes not from the Father but from the world" (1 Jn 2:16). The world that John refers to is, of course, not the world of people (see John 3:16) or the created world (see John 17:24), but the world or realm of sin (see James 4:4).

The goal or ultimate aim (purposed end) of every creature must be related to its beginning cause, its Creator, for "the Lord works out everything for his own ends" (Prv 16:4). His plan for us human creatures is for us to conform consciously to his will; and "it is God's will that you should be sanctified" (1 Thes 4:3). "Just as he who called you is holy, so be holy in all you do; for it is written: 'Be holy because I am holy'" (1 Pt 1: 15-16).

Let us pause and ask: Are we running in the right direction?

Opportunity Knocking

78

The sad tale is told of a shipwrecked man who spent months alone on an island, scanning the horizon daily, hoping for a ship to pass nearby. When a cruise ship finally came in sight he was recognized from a distance as a survivor, and a rescue party was immediately launched. But suddenly ashamed of his tattered clothes and unshaven face, the man hid from his would-be rescuers, as they called and searched for him in vain. With their hopes dashed, they returned to the ship. His hopes also dashed, the survivor fell to his knees in the sand, weeping at his lost opportunity.

The story epitomizes the mentality of persons who would like to escape from the bondage of sin, but are ashamed of what others might think of them if they admitted their weakness and failures. Similarly, some recognize a void in their life, but are afraid or are unwilling to pay the price of filling that void. Such was the rich young man in the gospel who heard the call of Christ, but wasn't prepared to make the sacrifice required to follow the call.

Refusal to come to grips with a real conversion of heart—a *metanoia* of the soul—is a form of the bondage that Jesus spoke about: "Everyone who sins is a slave to sin... A slave has no permanent place in the family" (Jn 8:34-35). Nothing is more morally enslaving than to become addicted to sin. But the "Great Emancipator" is always ready to liberate any humble penitent: "If the Son sets you free, you will be free indeed" (v. 36).

When God Smiles

Alone and defenseless, surrounded by a screaming, racist mob at the door of a North Carolina schoolhouse in 1962, an eight-year-old black girl looked up and began to smile. A woman shouted at her, "Hey, you little n——, what are you smiling at?"

"At God," she replied. "I see him up there smiling at me." The woman looked up, then at the girl. And the taunting ceased.

If we could see God smiling upon us lovingly in the midst of our adversities, how easily we could bear even the most arduous and painful trials. When we see only our hurtful situations, we find little to smile about. But God sees our goodness in submitting to his permissive will that permits the hurt in those situations. And his smile is a smile of love that is planning our great reward.

The apostles, after being flogged, *rejoiced* "because they had been counted worthy of suffering disgrace" (Acts 5:41). They must have been somehow aware of God smiling on them, as they left the Sanhedrin with enigmatic smiles, themselves "rejoicing."

And possibly they reminisced about the beatitude of Jesus: "Blessed are those who are persecuted because of righteousness.... Blessed are you when people insult you, persecute you and falsely say all kinds of evil against you because of me. *Rejoice and be glad*, because great is your reward in heaven" (Mt 5:10-12).

Don't Cross off the Cross

80

As every writer well knows, an editor will often cross out an irrelevant phrase as a journalistic blunder. Jesus, our divine Editor, crosses out, by his cross, our moral blunders called sins. However, having Jesus cross out our sins is not enough. We must be sure not to "cross off his cross" by refusing to take up our own cross *willingly* like Jesus. Our Lord warns: "Anyone who does not take his cross and follow me is not worthy of me" (Mt 10:38).

Our bill of debt was nailed to the cross by Jesus, who "made a public spectacle of [the powers of evil], triumphing over them by the cross" (Col 2:14-15). The cross is thus the symbol of Christianity—the vehicle, so to speak, of our redemption. But it is also the prototype of every Christian's suffering, for all are called to "share Christ's sufferings" (1 Pt 4:13, NAB). Hence, to refuse to take up one's cross is to refuse the Christian obligation and privilege to "participate in Christ's sufferings."

Jesus has said that life's crosses are unavoidable (see John 16:33), but that we can choose to refuse to bear those crosses *willingly*, and thus be unworthy of being Christians. If you're tempted to "cross off the cross," prayerfully walk with him "who for the *joy* set before him endured the cross" (Heb 12:2).

The Politics of Corn, Codfish, and Cranberries

In 1677, a century before American independence, the Massachusetts Colony enraged King Charles II by coining their own currency, the pine tree shilling. To smooth the ruffled royal feathers, colony leaders sent the king a gift of three of their choicest local products: Indian corn, codfish, and cranberries.

History is replete with events spawned by the ravaging effects of anger, in the form of economic retaliation, violent retribution, and even internecine wars. Less frequently, efforts to subdue the anger of a protagonist have been fortuitous, as "wise men turn away anger" (Prv 29:8). It has not always been by means of peace offerings such as corn, codfish, and cranberries; more often it has been accomplished with calming words and disarming love, for "a gentle answer turns away wrath" (Prv.15:1).

When anger is so controlled that it is directed *exclusively* against the evil behavior and not the evil person (a most delicate distinction requiring exquisite maturity), it is called "righteous indignation"; that was the anger Jesus expressed in casting the money changers from the temple. Meekness checks our anger against the offender *as a person*, but it also enables us to bear any insult from that offender, and to "turn the other cheek"; in that sense, we must learn to imitate "the meekness and gentleness of Christ" (2 Cor 10:1), who said, "Learn from me, for I am gentle and humble in heart" (Mt 11:29). Let us pray for that grace.

82

In earthquake-prone California, some jittery residents have a new twist on their prayer for faith. They no longer pray for faith that moves mountains, but for faith that the mountains won't move.

Our generation may well be the most insecure generation in human history. Widespread crime, new diseases, global ecological pollution, the worldwide threat of nuclear, biological, or chemical warfare, the escalating frequency and severity of climactic crises and catastrophes are all threats that make modern life insecure.

Spiritual maturity alone enables the soul to rely on a loving God more than on wariness or protective technology: "The eternal God is your refuge, and underneath are the everlasting arms" (Dt 33:27). With David's trust in God we can say, "I will lie down and sleep in peace, for you alone, O Lord, make me dwell in safety" (Ps 4:8).

King Solomon wrote: "Death is the destiny of every man" (Eccl 7:2). But even death holds no terror for the spiritually secure, who, like Job, have learned how to trust in God's love. "Though he slay me, yet will I hope in him" (Jb 13:15). Jesus' words remove death's sting: "He who believes in me will live, even though he dies" (Jn 11:25).

Rest secure. "He grants sleep to those he loves (Ps 127:2).

Topsy-Turvy Thinking

It was a moment of humor that could have originated only in the ingenuousness of a child's mind. A little girl asked, "Mommy, why does it get dark outside every time I put my pajamas on?"

Cause-effect relationships are not always apparent to a child. Neither are adults exempt from faulty thinking, sometimes in matters that have to do with the welfare of their very souls. We all know of people who neglect church attendance because of a falling-out with their pastor, thus blaming him for their own free choice to rupture their relationship with God. And countless immature, self-righteous people feel that they have a "right" to harbor resentment and withhold forgiveness because they were victimized unjustly, or because the offender hadn't apologized.

Such petty-minded individuals—many of whom regard themselves as Bible-believing Christians—have never been impacted by the biblical injunction: "Your attitude should be the same as that of Christ Jesus: who,… taking the very nature of a servant,… humbled himself" (Phil 2:5-8). Their twisted thinking does not admit of Christlike self-sacrificing love and humility; their topsy-turvy mind cannot desire "being like-minded, having the same love… in humility considering others better than yourselves" (vv. 2-3).

"I have set you an example," said Jesus. "Now that you know these things, you will be blessed if you do them" (Jn 13:15, 17).

84

A little-known ecological tragedy was recently discovered by ornithologists: Some song birds are
breeding less and thus nearing extinction because
traffic noise drowns out their mating calls.

Love-communication is ineffectual if it is not
heard. For those who truly "know" him, God's love-
calls are heard in spite of the abounding raucous nois-
es of worldly distractions. "His sheep follow him
because they *know* his voice. But they... do not recognize a stranger's voice" (Jn 10:4-5).

Yet it is not enough to know the shepherd's voice.
Each sheep must also learn to know the shepherd
himself: Among humans, one cannot fall in love with
a voice—even though it is recognized or "known." It
is only possible to love a *person*—when that person is
known. "I know my sheep and my sheep know *me*"
(v. 14). This "personal knowing" of the Lord is salvif-
ic for those who are aware of its necessity: "This is
eternal life: that they may *know* you, the only true
God, and Jesus Christ, whom you have sent" (Jn
17:3).

"Knowing" the voice in the love-call leads to a
"knowing" of the divine caller. Only then can we go
on to truly love him. Jesus, while praying to the
Father, explains this divine dynamic: "Righteous
Father, I have made you *known* to them... in order
that the *love* you have for me may be in them and that
I myself may be in them" (Jn 17:25-26). That's how
we "fall in love with God."

Fat Cat Leaves a Caboodle

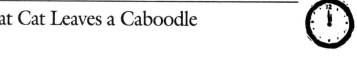

Oregon's richest cat has gone to the big litter box in the sky—and left the town of Tangent $250,000 richer. Twelve years ago Kitty Cat Bass inherited owner John Bass' five-bedroom farmhouse, lived there until her nine lives were up, and then left the estate to the city, as the deceased owner's will stipulated.

Even a kitty "has not a lasting city" (Heb 13:14 NAB). The wealthiest "fat cat" in your nearby upscale neighborhood will eventually have to leave all his material goods as he is stripped of everything by the grim reaper. At every funeral we are reminded by the remains in the casket that "you can't take it with you." Or, as the old bromide has it, "There are no pockets in a shroud."

It helps to recall the parable about the materialist who built bigger barns for his accumulated wealth. God said to him. "You fool! This very night your life will be demanded from you." Jesus concludes: "This is how it will be with anyone who stores up things for himself *but is not rich toward God*" (Lk 12:16-21).

Providing a "nest egg" for one's future is not bad (otherwise buying insurance would be sinful, as would pension provision). But storing up riches without being "rich toward God," says Jesus, is a stupidity great enough to deserve the epithet, "You fool!" "Provide purses for yourselves that will not wear out," he urges, "a treasure in heaven that will not be exhausted" (Lk 12:33).

86 Doctors took one look at the x-rays of a teen who'd been suffering from headaches and hallucinations all her life, and found that the cause was all in her head. It was a bullet lodged in her brain! The seventeen-year-old from Limoges, France, had been hit by a hunter's stray bullet when she was a baby. Her mother had noticed the bleeding head wound, which the doctor simply bandaged up. Unfortunately, it's now too risky to remove the slug.

"Some people have all the luck" is a phrase we often hear. It's used by many who forget that not all luck is good luck. Everyone knows of persons who are handicapped from infancy through their entire life, like the girl with a bullet in her brain. What is often forgotten is that "luck"—good or bad—is a misnomer for Divine Providence. And only in the light of Providence is "luck" always good. "'I know the plans I have for you,' declares the Lord, 'plans to prosper you and not to harm you'" (Jer 29:11).

When we are under an avalanche of grief, the Lord sees it quite differently: "'Though the mountains be shaken and the hills be removed, yet my unfailing love for you will not be shaken'… says the Lord who has compassion on you" (Is 54:10).

For the countless persons who have never gone to bed with a full stomach, or never known a pain-free day in their lives, the Lord has a recompense planned that will stagger them—eternally.

Not a Chance

A pastor's informal Sunday morning survey of his congregants revealed that within the previous six months 20 percent of them had participated in some form of gambling—horse racing, lottery, etc. Later discussion exposed an underlying hope for a chance windfall, while avoiding the discipline of work, saving, and budgeting. These people had paired themselves with a materialistic monster called "More."

Paul's classic words to Timothy would be the perfect response to that situation: "Godliness with contentment is great gain. For we brought nothing into the world, and we can take nothing out of it... People who want to get rich fall into temptation and a trap and into many foolish and harmful desires that plunge men into ruin and destruction. For the love of money is the root of all evil. Some people, eager for money, have wandered from the faith and pierced themselves with many griefs" (1 Tm 6:6-10).

Paul's ideal puts most of us to shame: "I have learned the secret of being content in any situation, whether well fed or hungry, whether living in plenty or in want" (Phil 4:11-13). If we mastered that mentality, it would change almost every aspect of our society, from the abuses of public welfare funds to the need for parish bingo.

To Grow Up, Grow Down!

88 On Trinidad lives a frog that is a foot long as a tadpole. As an adult it shrinks until it's a little over an inch long.

As one matures or "grows up" spiritually, he or she "grows down" in humility, as God's word so often attests: "Whoever humbles himself like this child is the greatest in the kingdom of heaven" (Mt 18:4). "If anyone wants to be first, he must be the very last, and the servant of all" (Mk 9:35). "Humble yourselves before the Lord and he will lift you up" (Jas 4:10; see 1 Peter 5:6).

Humility is called the "authenticating virtue." St. Augustine in his *Spiritual Diary* writes: "Humility is the foundation of all the other virtues. In the soul in which this virtue does not exist, *there cannot be any other virtue except in appearance.*"

Mary in her *Magnificat* canticle acknowledged that the Lord had been "mindful of the humble state of his servant," and that he "scattered those who are proud... but has lifted up the humble" (Lk 1:48, 51-52). In Jesus' own words, "Everyone who exalts himself will be humbled, and he who humbles himself will be exalted" (Lk 14:11; 18:14). Repeatedly God's word promises grace to the humble (see James 4:6; 1 Peter 5:5). If we don't humble ourselves, God will do it for us. The upshot will be not humility but humiliation—to the extreme.

On the Carpet

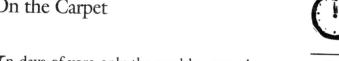

In days of yore only the wealthy owned carpets. Hence to be summoned by a rich boss was to be "called on the carpet."

In biblical terms, to be "called on the carpet" is to give an account of your management (see Luke 16:2). In many offices and workplaces, companies lose fortunes from workers' extended "water cooler chats." But in God's "company" there is strict accountability; we'll never "get away with" *anything*—from time wasting to theft, from padded expense accounts to dalliance with lustful thoughts, from neglect of one's children's sex education to cheating on one's income tax.

This doesn't make the Lord a "spy in the sky" snooping on us, but a just and exacting God, who "will reward everyone for whatever good he does" (Eph 6:8)—including repentance for one's failures, for his accounting demand is clothed in his mercy. After saving the adulteress from being stoned to death, when she was "on the carpet," he didn't condemn her, but he did say, "Go now and leave your life of sin" (Jn 8:11).

Being "called on the carpet" by the Lord means being given an opportunity to correct ourselves. Only those who reject his mercy will feel his punitive justice, says Aquinas. "A bruised reed he will not break" (Mt 12:20; Is 42:3). Let us stand "on the carpet" now, before judgment day, when "each of us will give an account of himself to God" (Rom 14:12).

Wishing "Well"

90 Throwing coins into a wishing well is a superstition intended to reinforce one's "wishing" for something good to *happen*. That is a far weaker human act than being "willing" to *do* something good. If every wishing well were a "willing well," we'd have a better world.

Philosophers distinguish between volition and velleity. Volition is a clear intent of the will; velleity is a conditioned wish. Volition says, "I will do it." Velleity says, "I would do it—if"; or, "I would like to do it." Webster's dictionary defines velleity as "a wish that does not lead to the slightest action."

What did Jesus mean when he said, "The kingdom of heaven has been forcefully advancing, and forceful men lay hold of it" (Mt 11:12)? He meant that the wishy-washy "wishing" type, who are not the true "willing" type, will not inherit the kingdom of heaven. To be a true disciple of Christ requires spiritual courage, vigor, power, and determination—volition, not mere velleity.

Jesus had to rouse his apostles out of their torpor at a time when they needed extra willpower to fight temptation. "The spirit indeed is willing," he said, "but the flesh is weak" (Mt 26:41, RSV). He needs followers with their "face set like flint" (Is 50:7), who heed Paul's words: "Stand firm... Always give yourselves fully to the work of the Lord... Your labor is not in vain" (1 Cor 15:58).

First Things First

The tiny daughter of a businessman wandered away from him at a shopping mall, and was lost for several hours. Later, her father told his friend, "I had urgent office work to be done, but I couldn't even begin to think of that during those torturous hours. I could only pray, 'God, my child is lost; help me find her!' At that time God's grace enabled me to feel a tiny bit of the divine anguish that our heavenly Father feels when a soul wanders away from him."

All of God's many concerns regarding his creation are light compared to the urgency of his desire to save even one soul: "God our Savior wants all men to be saved and to come to a knowledge of the truth." How do we know this is God's greatest concern? Because he paid the ultimate price to attain it: he "gave *himself* as a ransom for all men" (1 Tm 2:6). And his redemptive motive is touching: "He rescued me because he delighted in me."

Think again about the anguished love of the man whose daughter was lost in the mall, and its analogy with God's love. How can it be that God regards my soul and every soul as precious, and yet I can regard it so casually? God's exquisite love for souls should be replicated in my zeal for my own soul and that of others. All who are precious to him should be precious to me.

Hold on to my hand, Lord, and use me to reach out to others.

Pray It Again, Sam

92 Neglecting to join in the usual family grace before meals, a young lad began eating while the others prayed. Asked to explain himself, he said, "It's all left-overs; it's already prayed over."

You'd think that praying for something once would be enough, since God isn't hard of hearing. Jesus said, "When you pray, do not keep on babbling like pagans, for they think they will be heard because of their many words. Do not be like them, for your Father knows what you need before you ask him" (Mt 6:7-8).

It is true that Jesus condemned repetition in prayer, but only *vain* repetition by those who "think they will be heard because of their many words" (lip service), rather than prayer from the heart, for "out of the overflow of the heart the mouth speaks" (Mt 12:34). And he quoted Isaiah 29:13: "These people honor me with their lips, but their hearts are far from me. They worship me in vain" (Mt 15:8). Vain repetition is vain worship.

But there is a noble form of repeated prayer that shows a calm, reverent, but ongoing dependence on God for an answer. Jesus spoke of that in his parable of the widow repeatedly importuning the judge for justice until she succeeded. He prefaced the parable by explaining that it was "to show them that they should always pray and not give up" (Lk 18:1). God never tires of hearing us repeat, "I love you, Lord. In your love for me, hear my prayer."

Sales Resistance, Advanced Course

Pesky telephone salespersons, who usually call at dinnertime, can be dealt with creatively. Agree to buy whatever they're selling, but say that you must first check with the executor of your bankruptcy case. Or ask for the caller's number, saying that you'll call back a little later. When you have the number, tell the caller to expect your return call sometime after midnight.

Intrusions into our daily plans seem to be an unavoidable problem for most people. But not all intrusions are obnoxious. We *want* to be notified when there's a family emergency, or a change of a scheduled appointment. And one form of "intrusion" we should never resent is a silent nudge of grace through which God often manifests his will for us. Such "nudges" are called actual graces—as distinguished from "sanctifying" or "habitual" grace, which is a holy sharing by which we "participate in the divine nature and escape the corruption in the world caused by evil desires" (2 Pt 1:4).

Actual graces, theologians tell us, are intended to enlighten our mind about spiritual or moral matters, or to strengthen our will to do good and avoid evil. Thus, the Holy Spirit "intrudes" in our prayer: "The Spirit helps us in our weakness. We do not know what we ought to pray for, but the Spirit himself intercedes for us with groans that words cannot express" (Rom 8:26).

Holy Spirit, if you call at dinnertime or any time, it's OK.

94

Maintaining an exercise regimen is never easy, but one comedian proposed a unique form of motivation. He suggested that exercise-resistant couch potatoes could motivate themselves to do frequent sit-ups by placing the TV remote control between their toes!

Motivation is the basic success factor for everything we do, but it is more complicated than we might imagine. Psychologists think that the average human decision may be sparked by as many as eight different conscious or subconscious motives simultaneously. In a well-integrated personality, these are properly subordinated, with more selfish interests at the bottom of one's "value scale."

What is the highest possible human motivation? It relates to the ultimate purpose of human existence, namely, the glory of God. Hence, Paul highlights the optimum motivation for even the most prosaic actions: "Whether you eat or drink or *whatever you do*, do it all for the glory of God" (1 Cor 10:31).

All subhuman creatures, whether they be rocks, roses, or rats, give "material" glory to God by their very existence, which they derive from him. But "formal" glory can be given to God only by a sin-free act of a free will that knowingly intends to praise (that is, "compliment") him as the "be-all and end-all" of creation. "*Whatever* you do, whether in word or deed, do it all in the name of the Lord Jesus, giving thanks to God the Father through him" (Col 3:17).

When All Else Fails...

The secretaries' lounge at NASA has a wall poster **95** that reads: "Women astronauts are indispensable. If the crew is lost in space, *somebody* has to ask for directions!"

It seems axiomatic that men, in general, are more reluctant to ask for directions than women are; a motto for such men might be the one emblazoned on my humorous desk plaque: "If all else fails, follow directions." Those who neglect to read directions on road signs, exams, or medicine bottles are no better off than those who are *unable* to read them.

The best direction is given by example, like the driver who says, "Follow my car; I'll lead you there." Jesus gave that kind of direction: To attain peace, he said, "Learn from me,... and you will find rest for your souls" (Mt 11:29). To practice charity, he said, "I have set you an example that you should do as I have done" (Jn 13:15). For directions in coping with suffering, Peter says, "Christ left you an example, that you should follow in his steps" (1 Pt 2:21). For a Christic attitude, Paul says, "Your attitude should be the same as that of Christ Jesus" (Phil 2:5). And John adds: "Whoever claims to live in him must walk as Jesus did" (1 Jn 2:6). Jesus' true followers are Jesus imitators.

His directions are caught, not taught, by "osmosis." Reading the Gospels is how we *absorb* "the mind of the Lord" (1 Cor 2:16).

96 A young lady told her pastor she was "fed up" with her work environment. She was the only one there with any religious ideals, and wanted to quit. He asked her, "Where do you put the lamps in your house?" Taken aback by the question, she responded that they would be placed in otherwise dark areas. Her own mind was enlightened by her very answer to that question. His question was a one-sentence thought-provoking commentary on Christ's words: "Let your light shine before men, that they may see your good deeds and praise your Father in heaven" (Mt 5:16).

"Lighting a candle" may be as simple as lighting up one's face with a smile when it's difficult, or a word of encouragement to a downcast coworker; it may be the example of a brief "Bible-snack" during one's lunch hour, or a clear answer to a spiritually or morally confused employee. "In *everything* set... an example by doing what is good," is Paul's simple advice (Ti 2:7). That "everything" embraces a myriad of opportunities that present themselves to us daily for a prudent and loving response.

Try out Paul's checklist of good example opportunities: "in speech, in life, in love, in faith and in purity" (1 Tm 4:12).

A Time to Pray, a Time to Play

Imagine losing a soccer game by one goal—scored in the *first three seconds* of the game! At the very opening of a game in Brazil, the Corinthians scored the game's only goal while the goalie for the Rio Preto team was still on one knee, praying for victory!

There's a time to pray and a time to play, a time to be still and a time to act (see Ecclesiastes 3). Moses had to learn that principle. When he was waiting and praying for God to protect his flock from Pharaoh's charging army, the Lord said to Moses, "Why are you crying out to me? Tell the Israelites to *move on...* so they can go through the sea on dry ground" (Ex 14:15-16).

All prayer is good. We are even told to "pray continually" (1 Thes 5:17)—not, of course, by continual formal prayer; the term "continually" means that a spirit of prayer must permeate all we do. But there are times when formal prayer would be out of place and contrary to God's will. It would be wrong for a mother to be praying in church at a time when her family needs her at home to prepare their dinner. God made Moses adjust his prayer timing. It took a soccer game defeat to teach that to a goalie.

Both the timing and the object of prayer are Spirit-inspired: "We do not know what we ought to pray for, but the Spirit himself intercedes for us... in accordance with God's will" (Rom 8:26-27).

Eat My Dust!

98

That old fabler Aesop had a good grasp of the self-deceit in self-aggrandizement. He wrote: "The fly sat upon the axletree of the chariot wheel and said, 'What a dust do I raise!'"

The first effect of arrogance is self-deception, as the word of God reminds us: "The pride of your heart has deceived you" (Ob 3). In the eyes of God, "arrogance is like the evil of idolatry" (1 Sm 15:23); hence, "the Lord detests all the proud of heart" (Prv 16:5). Were it not so evil, haughtiness would make one as laughable as the hoity-toity fly on the chariot axle.

But self-deceit is not the only spin-off effect of insolence. It leads to something far more heinous—the sin of "presumption." Presumption, as a sin, is pridefully presuming that one can attain holiness and even salvation by merely using one's free will, under law, without any need for God's grace—the heresy of Pelagianism.

Living as if there were no need of God and his supporting grace is the greatest folly: "He who trusts in himself is a fool" (Prv 28:26). Jesus directed his parable of the Pharisee and the publican to those "who were confident of their own righteousness" (Lk 18:9). To show the seriousness of this, Scripture says that this mentality causes one to lose all grace formerly accumulated: "If... he trusts in his righteousness and does evil, none of the righteous things he has done will be remembered" (Ez 33:13).

Faith in Fact Is Faith in Act

Leading his congregation in prayer, a minister in a country church in the Ozarks uttered a petition that must have given the angels food for thought. "Dear Lord, if you can't make us hold much, at least make us overflow."

Either a small or large container can overflow. Most of us, when faith-challenged, find that our "faith container" doesn't seem to hold much—not enough to move mountains, anyway. But no matter how small our faith may be, still it can "overflow" in good works. In fact, our love-motivated good works increase our faith, and also show its authenticity, as James asserts (see James 2:14-26).

Faith without works, he says, is dead (2:17); the tree of faith without the fruit of good works is a dead tree. Though it may give assent to doctrinal truths, it will not pass muster on the day of judgment if it doesn't bear the first *fruit* of the Spirit—love (Gal 5:22), a love expressed in works of charity.

How does faith "overflow" in works of love? By faith we truly *believe* in our heart that it is Jesus we serve in even the least of his brethren (see Matthew 25:40). And this faith overflows at three levels. First by providing material needs for others, like food and clothing; second, by nonmaterial help, such as instruction or encouragement; and third, by nourishing them with grace, e.g. by prayer or good example. This is the triple overflow of faith.

Go with the Flow

100

Have you ever tried going up a "down" escalator. Even if you make it to the next floor, you'll be exhausted.

We spend too much time and trouble going the wrong direction on life's one-way streets, or swimming against the current. It's so much easier (and safer) to "go with the flow." But the surprising thing is that the Lord himself provides the "flow"—he takes the initiative in countless episodes of grace (theologians call this "prevenient grace"). Recognizing God's initiative in all our spiritual endeavors is essential. Jesus says, "No one can come to me unless the Father... draws him" (Jn 6:44). If anyone is seeking God, then it is God who is at work in him.

To cultivate the awareness of and appreciation of God's love in taking this initiative, ponder these five scriptural truths:

1. God is always at work around you (see Psalm 139:7-10).

2. God pursues a continual love relationship with you (see Jeremiah 31:3).

3. God invites you to join him in his work (see John 6:28-29).

4. God reveals himself, his purposes, and his ways (see John 15:15).

5. God lets you experience him as you submit to him (see Ephesians 3:17-19)

Bright As Night?

The ancient Celts recognized only two seasons in the year—light and dark—somewhat like Eskimos above the Arctic circle with "midnight sun" in summer and long dark days in the winter.

In the spiritual life there are likewise only two seasons—light and darkness. Paul writes of both day and night in the same sentence to counterpoint the difference between spiritual enlightenment by faith in Jesus and the spiritual darkness that envelops those refusing to believe in him. For those not living with the Lord, even "the *day* of the Lord will come like a thief in the *night*" (1 Thes 5:2).

As if consoling children afraid of the dark, Paul reminded the Thessalonians—whom he had complimented on their vibrant faith, hope, and love (1:3)—that those very virtues were a sign that they "belong to the day" (5:8): "You… are not in darkness so that this day should surprise you like a thief. You are all children of the light and… of the day. We do not belong to the night or to the darkness. So then, let us not be like others, who are asleep, but let us be alert… For God did not appoint us to suffer wrath but to receive salvation" (5:4-6, 9).

Thus, if we are truly "children of light" we need not fear the darkness of God's wrath in the coming day of the Lord.

What Can You Do with a "Birr"?

102 If I gave you a "birr," what would you do with it? If I were you, I'd cash it (in U.S. currency). It's Ethiopian money.

Just as the usefulness (subjective value) of a coin may vary in different situations, so also many human activities have considerable value in one situation but little or no value in another situation. For example, studying a Bible passage merely in order to be more intelligently involved in an upcoming Bible study session could well be fulfilling academically or socially, but spiritually it may be an act of little or no value. Yet reviewing that same Bible passage could be spiritually enriching and replete with rich spiritual insights, if it is done prayerfully and with a humble and loving yearning to know more about the Lord and his plans for one's salvation and sanctification.

Paul reminds Timothy that "the holy Scriptures are able to make you wise for *salvation*.... thoroughly equipped for every good work" (2 Tm 3:15-17). To study God's holy word only to acquire scholarly knowledge about it has, of course, some real value in the academe ("useful for teaching," Paul says in verse 16), but *by itself* that kind of encounter with God's word does not lead intrinsically either to one's own salvation or sanctification. God's love letter has countless *personal* messages for you. Have you found them?

Changing Your Outlook to an Uplook

At a metropolitan intersection a pollster sprang this question on twenty passersby: "Without looking up, tell me what the sky looks like right now." Not one could say. To most city people, the sky and its clouds are of little or no consequence.

To many of us, the heaven that awaits us "up there" is of little or no immediate consequence. We're content to wait until we get to heaven to get preoccupied with thoughts of it; we don't take time to "look up" from down here where earthly preoccupations compete for our attention.

Paul's imperative admonishes us clearly against this tendency: "Set your hearts on things above.... Set your minds on things above, *not on earthly things*" (Col 3:1-2). He then implies that this habitual "up-look" prepares us for the parousia: "When Christ... appears, then you also will appear with him in glory" (v. 4). He thus affirms Jesus' injunction to "lift up your heads" to await his "coming in a cloud with power and great glory" (Lk 21:27-28).

Elsewhere Paul proposes that same eschatological motive for fostering a spiritual uplook: "I say, even with tears, many live as enemies of the cross of Christ... Their mind is on earthly things. But our citizenship is in heaven. And we eagerly await a Savior from there, the Lord Jesus Christ" (Phil 3:18-20). His coming will make our earthly interests look like straw.

When the Obvious Isn't

Eyeglasses were used for four centuries before 1730, when a London optician named Edward Scarlett thought of anchoring them to the ears. Obviously, we're often slow to see the obvious.

One of the most obvious things that fail to be consistently obvious to most people is the simple fact that we all have to die sometime—except persons alive at the time of Jesus' second coming; they'll be instantly "reconfigured" (see 1 Corinthians 15:51-52).

Of course, the nearly universal law of death is obvious at funerals; all mourners probably wonder when they'll be "coffined" by the undertaker. But such mortality-awareness soon fades. If the almost universal law of death is so obvious, why doesn't it appear *consistently* obvious to us? Why doesn't that truth impact our every interest and decision in our daily life?

This need not be a morbid preoccupation with death, like a suicidal depression, but rather a joyful expectation: "My heart is glad and my tongue rejoices... because you will not abandon me to the grave" (Ps 16:9-10). An authentic Christian death-wish desires not escapism but fulfillment, as expressed by Paul: "I desire to depart and be with Christ" (Phil 1:23).

For the truly repentant person, falling in death can be beautiful... it's just falling into the arms of a loving God.

Bourbon with a Sermon

In old frontier towns the first ones to set up shop were whiskey sellers and preachers. Today, when neighborhoods are dying, the last places to shut down are liquor stores and churches. There has to be a moral in that demographic footnote.

Perhaps the moral is that eagerness to start and reluctance to depart are characteristics of powers of evil, but they're also characteristics of powers for good. Every spiritually beleaguered person feels like the rope in a tug-of-war, being pulled one direction by an enemy bent on the person's downfall, and pulled in the other direction by a spiritual Ally dedicated to the person's upbuilding. Intensity of purpose on both sides is what makes all spiritual warfare so ferocious and exhausting.

In the heat of spiritual combat, it's easy to forget that our battle has already been won—on Calvary twenty centuries ago. Our present struggle is mainly our faith-effort to claim the already won victory over the forces of evil: "You, dear children, are from God and have overcome them, because the one that is in you is greater than the one who is in the world" (1 Jn 4:4).

We can overcome, not by fighting, but by resisting: "Resist the devil, and he will flee from you. Come near to God and he will come near to you" (Jas 4:7-8). One bumper sticker says it quite aptly: "If you feel far from God, guess who moved!"

Try This Breath Test

Many church bulletins have popularized this "breath test": Hold this page near your face and blow on it. If it turns green, call your doctor. If brown, see your dentist. If purple, consult your local psychiatrist. If red, call your broker immediately. If yellow, arrange with your lawyer to prepare your will. If it remains the same color, you're in good health, so there's no reason why you should not attend church this coming Sunday.

Debunking poor excuses for any form of spiritual sloth could easily become a full-time job for any pastor. Instead of a "breath test," we all need to take a gut-level "honesty test" periodically to check our motives. The results may surprise us. For instance, is it *really* true that we don't have time for prayer or Bible reading? Do we *really* take seriously the obligation to tithe to the Lord's work? Is our forgiveness of our enemies *really* "from the heart" as Jesus commands? Do we *really* mean it when we say, "Thy will be done"?

Paul reminds us (see Romans 2:15-16) that our conscience may excuse us, but it may also accuse us, and that Jesus will judge us ultimately on the basis of the secrets of our conscience. One day "the thoughts of many hearts will be revealed" (Lk 2:35) by the "God who knows the heart" (Acts 15:8). On that day our feeble excuses will melt like wax in a blazing sun. It behooves us to surface our motives to our own conviction before the Lord does.

Where Were You when the Lights Went Out?

Centuries ago a European nobleman built a church to leave as a spiritual legacy for his townspeople. At the opening ceremony, the townsfolk began asking, "Where are the lamps? How will it be lighted?" The nobleman pointed to empty lamp brackets along the walls, each assigned to a family that was given a lamp to be brought and lighted at the worship service each Sunday—a striking reminder that failure to attend Sunday worship would thus leave part of God's house and God's people in darkness.

The clustering of persons that forms any community serves many deep sociological purposes, for Aristotle reminded us that humans are "political (social) animals." But God's revelation delineates far greater benefits of societal clustering when it is done for spiritual reasons. It not only provides the exercise of supernatural virtues like charity, compassion, patience, fortitude, kindness, and generosity, but it also occasions a very special modality of Christ's presence when even two or three are gathered in his name (see Matthew 18:20). Moreover, even minimal human clustering for petitioning God can draw down miracles from his hand: "I tell you that if two of you on earth agree about anything you ask for, it will be done for you" (v. 19). In prayer, one plus one equals far more than two.

Neglecting to "bring your lamp" to your Christian community will deprive part of God's people of your light—and his!

Don't Resuscitate—Exterminate

108 The genius of modern technology has found ways to repair most types of defective gadgets, from virus-diseased computers to the Hubble telescope and spacecraft toilets. But no one has yet found a way to straighten a crooked billiard cue. A warped cue can only be junked and replaced with a straight one. Many such things are easier (or less expensive) to replace than to repair or restore, whether it be tattered currency or worn-out refrigerators. (Did you ever try to launder a soiled Kleenex?)

This "replace-don't-restore" principle applies in some way to the spiritual life of the soul. That's why Scripture often uses the word "new" or "renew" in the context of spiritual change: "With regard to your former way of life, put off your old self, which is being corrupted by its deceitful desires, to be made *new* in the attitude of your minds; put on the *new* self, created to be like God in true righteousness and holiness" (Eph 4:22-24). Paul had previously described this new creation: "We are God's workmanship, created [anew] in Christ Jesus to do good works, which God prepared in advance for us to do" (2:10). (That last phrase can give us a *new* enthusiasm for good works; our tasks have been custom-assigned by Providence just for us.)

Note the challenge with the privilege: "You have taken off your old self with its practices and have put on the new self, which is being renewed in the image of its Creator" (Col 3:9-10).

Free Choice:
To the Church or the Gallows

The most incredible law that was ever established in the United States was one enacted by the state of Virginia in 1610; it prescribed not jail, but the *death penalty* for any healthy adult failing to attend church for three consecutive Sundays!

Legislators argued that this didn't infringe on one's freedom of religion (or lack of it), since everyone was free to choose church or the gallows. That could mean the freedom to choose to endure a boring sermon or to endure capital punishment (and not a few rebels hesitated over those alternatives!).

In our time the pendulum of civil liberty has swung to the opposite extreme—an extreme equally outrageous. Legal "freedom of choice" today smacks of libertinism—such as the freedom of choice in whether to kill an unborn infant. "Live as free men," says Peter, "but *do not use your freedom as a cover-up for evil; live as servants of God*" (1 Pt 2:16).

God respects our precious freedom, but hates our abuse of it, either by excess or by default: Those breaking "even the least of these [divine] commandments... will be called least in the kingdom of heaven," says Jesus (Mt 5:19). Yet he has a stronger condemnation for those seeking holiness by rigid human legalism: "Unless your righteousness surpasses that of the Pharisees,... you will certainly not enter the kingdom of heaven" (v. 20).

110

When "milking" a cobra for venom, it is not enough simply to avoid snakebite. Snake experts (technically called ophiologists) say that cobra venom is so toxic that merely handling it with unprotected hands can cause a person to fall into a coma.

Daily and even hourly we are bombarded with "take care" messages urging caution: "Don't Walk" signals flash at street intersections; skull-and-crossbones symbols leer at us from dangerous substance containers; TVs and radios blare forth protective procedures to follow in hurricanes, tornadoes, and earthquakes; warning messages are featured on cigarette packs. Yet emergency rooms and trauma centers are crowded with victims who neglected to follow such precautionary directions.

The spiritual dangers that surround us are far more serious than bodily ones, for "what good will it be for a man if he gains the whole world, yet forfeits his soul?" (Mt 16:26). No cobra poisoning could compare with the damage caused by the spiritual venom of the serpent in the Garden of Eden; the affliction it spawned has contaminated every subsequent generation with the toxin of inherited original sin. That serpent is still slithering around us, attempting to deepen the effects of original sin in each of us with personal sin. Meanwhile, Jesus still urges us: "Pray so that you will not fall into temptation" (Mt 26:41).

What to Do with a Dead Soldier

Dead soldiers are annoying, especially if you're in a hurry.

A "dead soldier," of course, is a colloquialism for a speed bump—an asphalt mound across a road where drivers are tempted to drive too fast. In school zones, "dead soldiers" keep kids alive.

We all need slow-down reminders—not just when driving, but also when driven—driven by the zillions of "hectivities" that distract us from our ultimate destination. We need to ease up on the gas pedal and apply the brake pedal more often. A prerequisite to spiritual awareness of God's loving providence is spiritual alertness. We need to "stop and smell the roses," but we must first "wake up and smell the coffee."

By alerting us with the many frustrating but life-enriching "dead soldiers" in our life's path, the Lord seeks to condition us, by grace, to hear his divine whispers. For example, stalled by gridlocked traffic, we might hear the Lord tell us to be resigned to his will in that delay, and to use it to pray for ourselves or for the victims of the accident that precipitated the traffic jam.

Frustrated people "do not understand God's plan" (Mi 4:12), like the Pharisees, who "rejected God's purpose for themselves" (Lk 7:30). In every "slow-down" event in life, from interrupted schedules to the sudden death of a loved one, God speaks to us.

112

English-speaking travelers abroad are often amused by signs in fractured English—like a sign by a swimming pool at a French Riviera hotel: "Swimming forbidden in the absence of the savior."

Before our smile dies away at the quaint translation of the word "lifeguard," there emerges, almost ineluctably, a spiritual significance hidden in the curious wording. Nothing, including swimming, should be done in the "absence of the Savior." That he will never be "absent" from us was revealed from the beginning in his very name—"Emmanuel," meaning "God with us" (Mt 1:23). This prophetic sign was first applied to Christ when it was given to Ahaz (see Isaiah 7:14).

The name "God is with us" was originally meant to convince Ahaz that God would "*rescue*" him from his enemies. The Hebrew phrase "God is with us" connoted not just his ongoing *presence*, but also his ever-present *protection* (see Numbers 14:9; Psalms 46:7)—an always-on-duty "lifeguard," if you will, ever ready to "save."

We don't claim to be "once saved, always saved." That could lead us to regard salvation as a "license for immorality" (Jude 4). At each sin-lapse, we need to shout to our "Lifeguard" to rescue us again; we need an always-on-duty, "God-with-us" Savior.

"Call to me and I will answer you," says the Lord (Jer 33:3), for "*I am with you always*, to the very end" (Mt 28:20).

Here's Lookin' at You

Microminiature technology has produced a video camera hidden in fancy sunglasses with a pinhole lens in the nose bridge and fine-wire cables snaking through the ear piece and shoulder strap to a belt power supply and belly bag recorder. It's a boon for security agents—and for those with less-noble motives as well!

Our best technology is nothing compared to the marvels of "God's hidden camera": "The eyes of the Lord are everywhere, keeping watch on the wicked and the good" (Prv 15:3). "Nothing in all creation is hidden from God's sight. Everything is... laid bare before the eyes of him to whom we must give account" (Heb 4:13).

For sinners, who would like to evade God's scrutiny, that truth is frightening, but for the righteous it's a blessing: "The eyes of the Lord range throughout the earth to strengthen those whose hearts are fully committed to him" (2 Chr 16:9) and "are on those... whose hope is in his unfailing love" (Ps 33:18).

It is tremendously consoling to know that God is always watching us to see when and how he can provide strength for us in our weaknesses, but it is even more consoling to know that his eyes are on us while we are doing good works or praying. "The eyes of the Lord are on the righteous and his ears are attentive to their prayer" (1 Pt 3:12, quoting Psalms 34:15). "Then your Father, who sees what is done in secret, will reward you" (Mt 6:6).

114 Over a flame, sugar melts but salt hardens. Heat will melt wax but harden clay. Hot water hardens eggs but softens potatoes.

Under the fiery anguish of trial and tribulation, some people are hardened and embittered against the God who allows them to suffer, while in similar situations others are softened into a "thy-will-be-done" loving embrace of his wisdom and providence. Some become "hard-boiled eggs"; others become "baked potatoes."

Most probably at this very moment you are experiencing a cross of some sort—a physical pain, like a backache, or a worry about a loved one, a family or marriage problem, a job insecurity, a false accusation, an overwhelming temptation, or something else. Ask yourself the incisive question: Are you a potato or an egg? That is, does your hardship "soften" you in a warm and generous love response to God's will in the situation, or does it "harden" you into disappointment, negativity, or perhaps even bitterness?

It has been said that life is a grindstone that can grind you down or polish you up. Every sickness, problem, pain, hardship, adversity, or tribulation can be used either as a stepping-stone or as a stumbling block. "'I know the plans I have for you,' declares the Lord, 'plans to prosper you and not to harm you, plans to give you hope and a future'" (Jer 29:11). *Only* for those attuned to God's word and his love, every hardship becomes a stepping-stone.

Happy Death-Day to You!

Among the elderly, death is often linked to birth-days—women often die the week after theirs; men, curiously, the week before.

Incidence or coincidence? Life is rife with many such unsolved mysteries, most of which pertain to the closing curtain of life's final act. When, why, and how are mysteries related to death's arrival. But the inevitability of death is a given. "Man is *destined* to die once, and after that to face judgment" (Heb 9:27).

On the issue of life, cutesy bromides abound. One of the most meaningful is: "Life is fragile—handle with prayer." Why is this aphorism so meaningful? Because of another maxim, from classical spirituality: "As a person prays, so will he live; as he lives so will he die; as he dies, so will he fare for all eternity."

As death approaches, if we are truly thinking persons (and still able to think), we may be given the grace to prioritize our values. Our mind may be filled with many gratifying memories of the virtues we have practiced during life; but there will also be regrets—about past moral failures, wasted time, and so on. One regret that will come to the foreground in our life-review will be the countless times that we could have easily prayed but didn't. To prepare for a holy demise, learn to "pray always," both "*now* and at the hour of our death." Then, "have a happy death-day!"

Where Were You in '62?

116 Saudi Arabia abolished slavery in 1962. Lincoln's Emancipation Proclamation abolished slavery in the United States exactly a century earlier. To us, that's ancient history.

And yet, we are still living under the scourge of slavery in some way, for Jesus proclaimed that all sin is a pernicious form of slavery: "I tell you the truth, everyone who sins is a slave to sin" (Jn 8:34). Peter stated, "A man is a slave to whatever has mastered him" (2 Pt 2:19)—a sobering thought for anyone with any addiction, including an addiction to sin (for sin itself is addictive). Even Paul, in acknowledging his weakness, wrote to the Romans, who were familiar with slavery, "I am unspiritual, sold as a slave to sin" (Rom 7:14). Yet he found freedom in Christ (8:2).

Just as some countries cling to slavery for centuries before repudiating it, we as individuals may cling to enslaving habits of sin, from gossip to adultery. Unless our soul is illumined by the Spirit's luminous grace, exposing the horrendous nature of sin as "a disgrace to any people" (Prv 14:34), we'll remain enslaved. "All wrongdoing is sin" (1 Jn 5:17), and recognizing it as such is itself a grace by which God seeks to enlighten a wayward soul: "You have set our... sins in the light of your presence" (Ps 90:8).

If you really hate being enslaved, try a "conscience survey." Then turn to Jesus to break your bondage of slavery to sin.

Bible-Snatching—
Thievery with a Halo?

From bookstores and libraries countless books are shoplifted every year, as you know. But guess which is stolen most? Right—it's the Bible—the Good Book that says, "Thou shalt not steal"!

This paradoxical situation manifests an all too common kind of conscience distortion—the moral heresy that "the end justifies the means"—that an evil act is acceptable if the ultimate purpose is good. This warped idea is the rationale for an endless array of sins: unethical business deals, euthanasia, abortion, genocide, "ethnic cleansing," and other atrocities far worse than Bible-swiping.

"An evil action cannot be justified by reference to a good intention," says St. Thomas Aquinas (*Dec. Praec.* 6). "One may not do evil so that good may result from it," says the *Catechism of the Catholic Church* (#1756, 1789). Thus, a desire to read the Bible doesn't entitle one to steal a copy. And desire to end a war doesn't entitle a country to atom bomb noncombatant civilians. Those "who suppress the truth… are *without excuse*" (Rom 1:18-20).

By usurping priestly functions for a "good motive," Saul sinned (see 1 Samuel 13:12); also in "glorifying God" by sacrificing forbidden spoil (15:21). Aaron's idolatry was to quell a rebellion (see Exodus 32:22-24). Mankind's first sin was for a "good intention"—to gain wisdom (see Genesis 3:6). Ever since, man has found excuses for sin.

"Cool" Fools

118 Statistically, each cigarette smoked shortens your life by five minutes—a form of "slow suicide." Every knowledgeable person knows that; that's why so many have recently kicked the habit. Yet teenage smoking is on the rise—especially among girls. The answer to the big question "why?" is not advertising but peer pressure.

Peer pressure is based on fear of rejection by "significant others"—very common among love-starved kids. This longing for "human respect"—the regard for human approval, is not bad, but when it contravenes God's will, "we must obey God rather than men" (Acts 5:29).

Because of human respect, halfhearted Christians hesitated to risk identification with the early Christian community (5:13). But Paul courageously surmounted human respect: "We dared to tell you his gospel in spite of strong opposition" (1 Thes 2:2).

Be always intrepid in the face of human opinion: "Whether they listen or fail to listen" (Ez 2:7), "do not be ashamed to testify about our Lord" (2 Tm 1:8). Whether by pro-life bumper stickers or saying grace publicly, be always *openly* Christian.

God's Geometry—Closed Circles

The general population is divided into two types—racehorses and turtles. Racehorses are always on the go, with "many irons in the fire," while turtles love peace and calm. They both experience some disorder in their lives that they need to overcome.

"God is not a God of disorder" (1 Cor 14:33) or of unfinished business. He wants us to learn the art of closing circles. The turtles must press onward vigorously to complete their tasks, while racehorses must not dissipate their energies in taking on too many tasks, which may leave some uncompleted.

To "close circles" it helps to think of every proper task as God-assigned: "It is the Lord Christ you are serving" (Col 3:24), and to heed the angel's warning to the church in Sardis: "I have not found your deeds complete in the sight of God" (Rv 3:2). And planning is important, as Jesus teaches in his story of the man planning to build a tower he's unable to complete (see Luke 14:28-30).

"Closing circles" may relate to all types of unfinished business: such things as delayed apologies or unpaid debts: "Give everyone what you owe him" (Rom 13:7). It may be a compliment that you neglected to express, or a long overdue confession. It may mean giving timely sex education to your children or adopting the biblically mandated practice of tithing, helping the poor, or tidying your house. "Closing circles" will "square" you with God.

120 In one of his "makes-you-wanna-think-about-it" squibs, the poet Robert Frost wrote, "The reason why worry kills more people than work is because more people worry than work."

Whether you work or not, if you worry, you're under stress. Enough books about worry and about stress have been written to fill a library. But the "Good Book" also has something to say about both of these topics, which, of course, are interrelated. Worry—not to be confused with calm concern—is stressful and is condemned by Jesus as a form of lack of trust in God. Everyone, especially worriers, should meditate frequently on his treatise in Matthew 6:25-34. Even reading it prayerfully anesthetizes worry.

A premiere method of relieving stress is prayer. Even agnostic psychiatrists are coming to recognize that fact, and prescribe it for their patients (unfortunately they also prescribe counterfeit forms of prayer, such as New Age forms of "meditation" that carry with them untoward spiritual side effects). True prayer is not self-focused but God-focused: "When you pray, go into your room, close the door and *pray to your Father*" (Mt 6:6).

A second biblical stress-reducer is surrender or commitment of oneself to God, which teaches the art of "letting go." Worriers would do well to live (not just read) the words of Proverbs 16:3: "Commit to the Lord whatever you do, and your plans will succeed."

The "Good Old Days" Are Still Here!

Collegiate survey takers now say that very few engineering students have ever seen a slide rule or even know what it is. In this cybernetic age math is done with calculators and computers.

Junkyards are graveyards for out-of-date things. Old items are usually regarded as worthless, except perhaps as collectibles or antiques. But some old things will not submit to a price tag. The Cheops pyramid of Egypt, after being around for nearly fifty centuries, is still a priceless architectural wonder of the world.

Jesus said that a kingdom-wise teacher is like a house owner "who brings out of his storeroom new treasures as well as old" (Mt 13:52). One of the many interpretations of this difficult passage is that we "New Testament" people of God must "bring out" or share Christ's "new revelation" as one that is not "added to the old" but renews it. This year's car model improves on last year's but maintains the basic structure and strength of the old model. "I have not come to abolish... but to fulfill" (5:17).

We must turn to the "old" revelation to understand the new. But the value of the old derives from its (prophetic) Christ-focus spelled out in the "new" Christian revelation. "These are the [Old Testament] Scriptures that testify about *me*" (Jn 5:39). The "good old days" were good, but our present time is better. We now have the resurrected Jesus not just prophesied about, but with us!

What's It Worth?

122 In one single hour in the United States, more steel is poured than all the gold ever mined in the history of mankind! If all gold ceased to exist, it wouldn't cause any drastic change in our society. But if steel suddenly ceased to exist, our entire society would collapse, with its machinery, its buildings, its cars, its bridges, its entire infrastructure. For that reason, the real value of something is determined not by the rarity of the commodity but by its basic *usefulness*.

Christianity really "works"! Its norms and proposed virtues always "work" for our betterment, here and hereafter. Take, for example, the usefulness or "workability" of prayer. Numerous tests have shown scientifically that prayer can accelerate plant growth. Prayer can cure animals. And even anonymous hospital patients (who, for test purposes, are unknown to the pray-ers) heal faster when prayed for, even when unaware that they are "prayer targets."

Or take, for example, the Christian virtue of surrender to God's will. In producing anxiety control in psychiatric patients, no psychotherapy "works" as effectively as the devout practice of the Christian virtue of holy abandonment to God's will. Again, no marriage counseling "works" as well as when each spouse devoutly allows Christ to "borrow one's heart" to love the other with. One of Christianity's biggest blessings is that it "works"—always!

Speak Up, Not Down!

This anonymous quatrain speaks worthy "thoughts to live by":

> A careless word may kindle strife;
> a cruel word may wreck a life.
> A bitter word may hate instill;
> a brutal word may smite and kill.
> A gracious word may smooth the way;
> a joyous word may save the day.
> A timely word may lessen stress;
> a loving word may heal and bless.

The term "forked tongue" need not always connote duplicity; it may connote speech options. The tongue may curse or bless. It may engage in gossip, or charitably redirect such conversation. It may take God's name in vain or call upon God in humble prayer. It may insult or compliment, lie or proclaim great truths. It may brag arrogantly of one's gifts, or it may acknowledge that "a man can receive only what is given him from heaven" (Jn 3:27). James suggests such alternatives in the use of speech (see James 3:10).

In his classic treatise on the use of the tongue, James makes a remarkable statement: "If anyone is never at fault in what he says, he is a perfect man" (3:2).

One wonders what percentage of the world's sins are "speech sins." Let's ask the Incarnate Word to bless our gift of speech.

The Scent of Love

124 The old-time movie comic W.C. Fields said that he "loved" children; "I have them for breakfast every day!" He admitted the truth of what Goethe, the German writer, once said: "Children, like dogs, have so sharp a scent that they detect everything—the bad before all the rest."

There are adults that children tend to avoid. Psychologists know that most children in an initial encounter have an uncanny intuition of being liked or not, even before a word is spoken. But also sensitive adults can "hear the silent dialect of love" and inner beauty in another's tone of voice, attitude, and courtesies.

We all like to be warmly accepted by others. To cause this we need a certain warmth in ourselves, for love is reciprocal, since "love spawns love." Loving makes you lovable. In order to acquire a personal inner warmth, we need to cultivate an acute awareness of that lovableness and intrinsic dignity in each human being that reflects God's image and likeness. "God is love. *Whoever lives in love lives in God, and God in him*" (1 Jn 4:16). When your love is God's own love pouring from within you, you are irresistible!

"As dearly loved children," says Paul, "live a life of love, just as Christ loved us and gave himself up for us as a fragrant offering… to God" (Eph 5:1-2). Goethe was right. Love can be "smelled" as the very fragrance of God from within our hearts.

The Longing of Belonging

Do you exchange holiday greeting cards with people you haven't seen for years? If so, this reinforces the theory that social attachment—the need to belong, found in every culture—is more than a desire; it's a drive as strong as self-preservation. Greeting card exchange is just one way we maintain social linkage.

Psychologists say that this need to belong has two aspects: 1) frequent, *positive* interactions with the same persons, and 2) a framework of long-term, stable caring and concern. "A *faithful* friend is a life-saving remedy," says the proverbialist (Sir 6:16, NAB).

In established relationships, rejection is more hurtful than in a casual relationship. Being emotionally unsupported for an extended time by a parent, friend, or spouse can arouse apathy, anxiety, loneliness, depression, and often suicide or crime. Thus, a bonding *can* become a bondage. Once established, relationships are not easy to break away from, even when recognized as socially or spiritually harmful, as in gangs, cults, abusive marriages, gay partnerships, adultery, incest, and so on. To belong *can* be wrong.

To avoid disasters, like a life-shattering divorce, test your relationships *early* in the game. "Let your acquaintances be many, but one in a thousand your confidant. When you gain a friend, first test him, and be not too ready to trust him" (Sir 6:6-7, NAB). Seek out truly faithful friends—and seek to *be* one!

Who Loses Eighty Pounds Getting Washed?

The Statue of Liberty loses eighty pounds each day by copper loss from annual rainfall. Each raindrop erodes only an infinitesimal bit of copper from Lady Liberty. But, as the dictum has it, "many bits make a big bite."

Little things can do great damage, either because they're disregarded or not noticed. "Catch for us the foxes, the *little* foxes that ruin the vineyards," says the Song of Songs (2:15). Long-neglected small failings can ruin the "vineyard" of our soul.

"There is sin that does not lead to death" (1 Jn 5:17), called venial sin. But, like refuse, if not disposed of, it can breed things far more obnoxious—possibly even eventual failure by mortal sin.

To risk, even remotely, the bankruptcy of one's immortal soul would be foolhardy. The "what-does-it-profit-a-man?" challenge of Jesus is applicable in the accumulating of the garbage of sin. Why? The problem with accumulating habitual smaller sins, like gossip, impatience, or occupation with worldly entertainment, is that, unlike failing by an occasional mortal sin, the soul is *often without remorse*—and that's a dangerous state; disaster is then not far away. But those found "trustworthy in a very small matter" (Lk 19:17), promises Jesus, will be given a superabundant reward.

Misleading Labels?

To the average English-speaking person, hardly any language would seem more "foreign" than Chinese. Yet some linguists claim that Chinese—in its structure, not script, of course—is closer to English than English is to its European parent languages.

Time and time again, reality checks reveal that things are not always just what they seem. We tend to judge by appearances, and hence we often misjudge—not just in linguistic differences but even in behavioral differences. If we could somehow take a "reality check," for instance, of a criminal's conscience, with all the subjective factors that go to determine "imputability"—that is, the actual moral responsibility in God's eyes—we might be surprised to find little or no malice in many (not all) cases.

Judging a person negatively when there is a considerable risk of misjudgment is called in moral theology "rash judgment"—the sin most frequently committed and the one least often confessed. We tend to put "labels" on people: "He's just a drunk." "She's a mean-spirited person." "That kid is a brat." Labeling others as bad, while ignoring our own evils, can boomerang: "You who pass judgment on someone else... are condemning yourself" (Rom 2:1).

Except for juridical judging required for society to function (see Deuteronomy 1:16), "let us stop passing judgment on one another" (Rom 14:13), "for judgment belongs to God" (Dt 1:17). And he's fair!

128 No chemical compound is more useful than salt. Incredibly, it has 14,000 industrial uses. And providentially, it's abundant.

When it comes to real usefulness in terms of what will count for all eternity, nothing compares to God's revealed word, as Paul told Timothy: "All Scripture is God-breathed and is *useful* for teaching, rebuking, correcting and training in righteousness, so that the man of God may be thoroughly equipped for *every* good work" (2 Tm 3:16-17). That sounds almost like a panacea!

But St. Augustine lists even more Bible bonuses. He likens it to a road map to heaven that shows us the most direct and secure road to get there. It also provides road signs of dangers and alerts us to enemy ambush areas enroute and hidden snares that threaten our soul. It points out refreshment places along the way. It provides strength for our labors, trials, and sufferings on our toilsome journey heavenward. We might add to Augustine's list: the Bible is useful for devotional prayer, for persuasive preaching, in healing and deliverance. What could be more useful than that?

Both scholars and peasants can find useful things in God's versatile word. In the quaint metaphor of St. Gregory the Great, "Holy Scripture is a stream of running water, where an elephant may swim and a lamb may walk without losing its footing." So no one has an excuse for neglecting God's awesome and useful word.

Let the Garbage Man Do It

One of the many barometers for measuring the state of the economy, say money-watchers, is the number of garbage collectors working at any time. The more we buy, the more trash we generate.

The divine economy can be calibrated by the same principle. The more affluent we become spiritually, the more we "put off our old self,... corrupted by its deceitful desires" (Eph 4:22; see Colossians 3:9). The richer we are in spirit, the more "soul garbage" we throw out.

To understand the dynamic of sin displacement— "disposal of soul garbage"—we must understand how growth in negative holiness (absence of sin) relates to growth in positive holiness (the life of virtue). Imagine a glass of water capped with a layer of dirty oil. Adding water to the glass displaces the oil. More water means less oil. The more virtue we acquire, the more sin we get rid of. "You must rid *yourselves*," writes Paul, "of all such things as... anger, rage, malice, slander, and filthy language" (Col 3:8).

The Lord's "garbage disposal" service is superefficient; its removal, first of all, is *total*: "The Lord... forgives *all* your sins" (Ps 103:2-3). Secondly, the garbage is *unreturnable*. (Have you ever seen your garbage after it has been removed?) "You... hurl all our iniquities into the depths of the sea" (Mi 7:19). "If... the wicked man... turns away from his sin,... *none of the sins he has committed will be remembered against him*" (Ez 33:14-16). That's garbage service!

To Be Upside Down, Get Right Side Up

130

As a child I once heard my mother say that she was going to make an upside-down cake. "How?" I asked. "Standing on your head?" Later, when I was more semantically mature, I understood the symbolic use of the phrase "upside down."

Early Christians were accused of having "turned the world upside down" (Acts 17:6 KJV). Christianity continues to have a profound impact on society's value system. Our personal values correspond to the four basic dimensions of human nature:

1. the mind (intellectual and emotional);

2. the physical (bodily features and activities);

3. the spiritual (soul-God relationship);

4. the social (human interdependence).

In all of these four dimensions there is normally a maturation or growth in our four-dimensional value system.

Besides being God, Jesus was human like us in everything but sin (see Hebrews 4:15); hence he grew in those four human dimensions: *"in wisdom and stature, and in favor with God and men"* (Lk 2:52). He prioritized the spiritual ("favor with God") dimension, and his early followers imitated that mandated value priority: "Seek first [God's] kingdom and his righteousness" (Mt 6:33). Reversing their own value system they "turned the world upside down." So can we!

Gumshoes Accuse—
Gum Chewers Lose

Since 1992 gumshoes (detectives) in Singapore are on the lookout for chewing gum, which is legally banned there. Its possession isn't punished, but importing it reaps a hefty fine and a year in jail.

When the punishment doesn't fit the crime, we regard it as an injustice. Shoplifters' penalties may be severe, while rapists or drug traffickers get slap-on-the-wrist sentences or early paroles. Such human inequities make us blanch with indignation. But it's comforting to know that the Lord's sanctioning is quite different, since "'My thoughts are not your thoughts,' declares the Lord" (Is 55:8).

First of all, amnesty is *always* available to culprits like you and me. Whether our infractions are serious or minor, *one simple act of true repentance brings total forgiveness* from a God whose penalty for sin is imposed only on those who refuse his tender and abundant mercy. "You are a forgiving God, gracious and compassionate, slow to anger and abounding in love" (Neh 9:17).

Second, even for the unrepentant, God's mercy tempers his justice, because he "sympathizes with our weaknesses" (Heb 4:15): "God, you have punished us less than our sins have deserved" (Ezr 9:13).

Like the good thief Dismas, who at the throne of the cross "stole paradise," let us too "approach the throne of grace with confidence, so that we may receive mercy and find grace" (Heb 4:16).

Nothing to Squawk About

132 One guruism with a moral impact—in a tickle-the-funny-bone context—is the sage advice: "Live your life in such a way that you wouldn't be ashamed to sell your parrot to the town gossip."

Less facetiously, but just as forcefully, God's word offers similar advice regarding edifying speech and behavior: "Do not let any unwholesome talk come out of your mouths, but only what is helpful,... that it may benefit those who listen" (Eph 4:29). Paul adds other norms for edification: "In everything set an example by doing what is good... Show integrity... and soundness of speech,... so that those who oppose you may... have nothing bad to say about us" (Ti 2:7-8). And Paul tells Timothy to "set an example for the believers in speech, in life, in love, in faith and in purity,... so that everyone may see your progress. Watch your life and doctrine closely. Persevere in them, because if you do, you will save both yourself and your hearers" (1 Tm 4:12-16).

"Edify the church,... build up the church," he wrote to neophyte Christians (1 Cor 14:4,12). "When you were pagans... you were influenced and led astray" (12:2). Having been poisoned by bad example, they were now to nourish others... with good example. "Live such good lives among the pagans that they may see your good deeds and glorify God" (1 Pt 2:12).

Ask yourself: Do I always edify others—and thus glorify God?

If You Were for Sale, How Much Would You Cost?

During certain periods in ancient Rome almost any male slave could be purchased for two jars of raisins. For some people, the value of a human being hasn't changed much since then. Women have sold their newborn babies for a fix of cocaine. And what value is attributed to an unborn baby about to be dismembered and trashed?

God values humans a bit differently: "What is man that you... care for him... and crown him with glory and honor?" (Ps 8:4-5). "'I have loved you,' says the Lord" (Mal 1:2). "You are precious and honored in my sight" (Is 43:4). "Though the mountains be shaken... my unfailing love for you will not be shaken" (Is 54:10). And one lovesome translation of Hosea 11:3 reads, "I caress you tenderly as one who nuzzles an infant to his cheek." If you heard God whisper these rapturous words in your ear, what price tag would you put on yourself? Remember, *they are his words!*

If we could maintain a grace-prompted awareness, based on divine revelation, of our worth as humans made to "the image and glory of God" (1 Cor 11:7), would we ever have an inferiority complex? Would we ever experience depression from rejection by others? Would we ever even think of suicide? Would we ever feel lonely or worthless? Could we ever regard human existence as meaningless? No matter how routine, would life ever be boring?

When your self-esteem plummets, listen to God's love-whispers.

Fighting or Uniting, Hand-to-Hand?

134 What is the oldest spectator sport? You're right if you answered "fights between humans." Whether wrestling, swordplay, fisticuffs, or gladiatorial trident-and-net contests, early sports were brutal, and often fatal to one or both of the contestants.

Aggression in the animal kingdom in predator-prey conflicts preserves ecological balance. But in human society, most aggression or hostility is simply violence—a liability, not an asset. Untrammeled aggression has inflamed wars, crime, murder, torture, child abuse, genocide, slavery, rape, arson, and other social disasters.

Although "man's anger does not bring about the righteous life" (Jas 1:20), there is a righteous anger or indignation, like the anger of Jesus in dispelling the money changers from the temple. Righteous anger or aggression differs from the sin of anger, which is contrary to meekness: "In your anger do not sin" (Eph 4:26; Ps 4:4). That balancing act requires redirecting anger away from the offender, whom we must love spiritually, to the offense itself.

To avert the just anger of God, we must redirect the energy of our malicious anger into a deep spiritual love for our enemies, while hating their sin. "The wrath [anger] of God is coming... [so] you must rid yourselves of... anger, rage, and malice" (Col 3:6, 8).

A recent survey showed that four out of five Americans would like to know the future, even if it meant knowing when they would die. Even more revealing were the reasons people gave for wanting this knowledge. One lady said, "If I knew I would die next week, I'd go out and spend all my money!" A broker said, "I'm interested mainly in the future of the stock market; I'm not too concerned about the date of my death."

St. Paul offers a wake-up call to those who are unconcerned about the reality of life after death: "If *only for this life* we have hope... we are to be pitied more than all men" (1 Cor 15:19). All of our hardships, trials, persecutions, adversities, and pains would be utterly meaningless if they had no relationship to an afterlife.

St. Alphonsus wrote in *Great Means of Salvation*, "Death is the time of truth: then do all worldly things appear as they are—vanity, smoke and dust." St. Augustine observed, "When it is a question, not of dying, but of being dead, then death may well be said to be bad for sinners and good for saints" *(City of God, 13)*—an observation that affirmed what St. John heard from heaven: "Blessed are the dead who die *in the Lord*.... They will rest from their labor, for their deeds will follow them" (Rv 14:13).

Inoculated with Love

136   University researchers have found repeatedly that persons who engage in charitable works have above-average resistance to colds and flu. And expanding compassion improves one's disease immunity. Even witnessing others' acts of compassion will increase one's store of immunoglobulin E, thus raising one's immunity to disease.

Remarkable as this finding is, there is a more important immunizing effect of loving compassion—namely, immunity to selfishness. Since the biochemistry of the human body was designed by God, it is not surprising that his own word reinforces this scientific fact with appropriate advice: "Do nothing out of selfish ambition or vain conceit, but in humility consider others better than yourselves. Each of you should look not only to your own interests, but also to the interests of others" (Phil 2:3-4).

Spiritual immunity against the common sin of selfishness and self-pity results from altruism, for love "is not self-seeking" (1 Cor 13:5). "Watch yourself, or you... may be tempted. Carry each other's burdens, and in this way you will fulfill the law of Christ" (Gal 6:1-2). "If you *really* keep the royal law found in Scripture, 'Love your neighbor as yourself,' you are doing right," says James (2:8). "Each of us should please his neighbor for his good, to build him up.... Even Christ did not please himself" (Rom 15:2-3). Trenchantly Paul sums up this immunity treatment: "Nobody should seek his own good, but the good of others" (1 Cor 10:24).

Grinch in a Law Book

Imagine skipping the entire Christmas season for one year. Now imagine it for 22 years! Starting in 1659, that was how long the celebration of Christmas was *against the law* in Massachusetts.

The stability of the entire economy of all Western nations is tied irrevocably to Christmas sales—which begin shortly after the "back-to-school" sales! The movie, TV, music, and entertainment industries depend on the celebration of Christmas for a staggering amount of their annual income. Postal rates would soar if Christ's birthday ceased to be celebrated. Our Western society would shrivel hopelessly if that Massachusetts law were ever reenacted. And yet the sacrilege of a Christ-less Christmas that is so widely celebrated today is a parody of the real thing.

"Put Christ back in Christmas," says the Christian bumper sticker. But to do this we must put Christ back in our very lives, without hypocrisy: "They claim to know God, but by their *actions* they deny him" (Ti 1:16).

Do we deny Jesus often by our actions—or by our lack of them?

138 It is the largest and most complex crypt ever discovered; it entombed about 50 sons of the 150 children that Rameses' concubines bore him while he reigned unrivaled as the pharaoh that confronted Moses in Egypt 3,200 years ago. It seemed almost like God's last laugh at the arrogant ruler, in allowing this recently discovered mausoleum to be unearthed during the construction of a parking lot.

"He has brought down rulers from their thrones" (Lk 1:52). For the sacrosanct locale of his family's bones and thrones to be asphalted over as a parking lot is an indignity that bespeaks the worth of worldliness in the eyes of God. The world gazes on the shriveled grandeur and opulence of Rameses' dynasty, unearthed by pick and shovel, and sees only remnant shards of his earthly power in thief-plundered tombs. The idolized lifestyles of the rich and famous inevitably crumble into the ash heap of history.

The only thing of truly lasting value in anyone's lifestyle is one's spiritual wealth—"of greater value than the treasures of Egypt" (Heb 11:26). Of course, earthly wealth and fame are not evil in themselves, but gifts of God to be used for his glory; thus money is not the root of all evil, but "*love* of money" (1 Tm 6:10). "Keep your lives free from the *love* of money and be content with what you have" (Heb 13:5.). Likewise, fame is not evil, for Moses, the humblest man of his time (see Numbers 12:3), was as famous as Rameses. "Where your heart is, there is your treasure!"

Don't Spike the Mike

In the 1920s, broadcast studio technicians feared their delicate microphones might fail if "spiked" with sudden surges of volume. So they asked a singer of that time, Vaughn de Leath, to keep her voice low and gentle. Thus originated the old-time style of singing, later popularized by Bing Crosby, called "crooning."

Softness and gentleness in demeanor, song, or speech carries its own form of soothing persuasiveness. It can accomplish things where raucous, blustering stridence will fail. "A gentle answer turns away wrath, but a harsh word stirs up anger," observed Solomon (Prv 15:1). You don't need a proverb, or even much life experience, to know that "a hot-tempered man stirs up dissension, but a patient man calms a quarrel" (15:18), for "a man of understanding is even-tempered" (17:27). Examples of this abound in Scripture: for example, Gideon calmed the anger of the men of Ephraim, and "their resentment against him subsided" (Jgs 8:3).

It requires little experience in human diplomacy to know that "the tongue of the wise brings healing" (Ps 12:18), for "a wise man's heart guides his mouth, and his lips promote instruction" (16:23). "A patient man has great understanding" (14:29), so he knows that his "calmness can lay great errors to rest" (Eccl 10:4).

Prayerfully read the book of Proverbs for consummate wisdom in using the heavenly strategy of meekness, especially in speech.

Where's the Fire?

140 The London fire department was called to douse a chimney fire in Luton Hoo, a stately mansion. Arriving, they saw two hundred chimneys. When they finally found the right one, the fire had already burned itself out.

Each day seems to have enough problems to keep us scurrying, but more often than not, after all our freneticism, many of these problems are like that chimney fire that burned itself out.

Martha was a biblical figure with whom most of us can readily identify; she was "distracted by all the preparations that had to be made." But Jesus gently led her to focus her scattered efforts and prioritize her goals: "Martha, Martha, you are worried and upset about many things, but only one thing is needed" (Lk 10:40-41).

Martha's sister, Mary, had focused on the *person* of Jesus, while Martha had focused on *things* to be done for Jesus. When first things are put in first place, secondary things seem to fall into place and almost take care of themselves, like harmless fires that burn out almost of their own accord. Jesus did not propose negligence or lazy passivity, but the seeking of priorities that somehow enable one to handle secondary matters more expeditiously. His great mandate to prioritize our goals was a simple injunction, but one that would change our whole lifestyle if implemented: "Seek first his kingdom and his righteousness [holiness], and all these things will be given you as well" (Mt 6:33).

Lobster à la Yuck!

The next time your wallet feels a little light and your dinner guest starts eyeing the "surf and turf" section of the menu, you might casually mention the fact that lobsters are taxonomically related to spiders. In colonial times, lobsters were regarded as worthless, and were fed only to slaves!

What appears elegant in one context can become repulsive in another. This becomes distastefully apparent, for instance, to missionaries who first observe African tribesmen relishing as a consummate "delicacy" the scooped-out guts of the giant buffalo beetle. Our world is replete with such vagaries of subjectivity.

This subjectivity relates not just to such things as gourmet food, but, more significantly, to individual consciences that have been formed or malformed by environment or culture. To conform subjective norms to true objective norms in matters of conscience requires a "base line" of morality—natural law— "law… written on their hearts, their consciences also bearing witness" (Rom 2:15). But for more problematic issues, more is needed: God's revealed truth.

But God's revelation—including his expressed will spelling out more detailed applications of natural moral law—is not yet widely known. Natural law says murder is evil; yet not everyone knows that this includes euthanasia, suicide, and abortion. We must "teach what is right" (Lk 20:21), but to avoid rash judgment, remember that ultimately, "it is the Lord who judges" (1 Cor 4:4).

The Jesus Lizard

142   The basilisk is a light-bodied, web-footed reptile that can run across vast stretches of water on its hind legs (as long as it doesn't stop). For this reason, the creature is sometimes called the "Jesus Christ lizard."

Of course, it might make more sense to call it "Peter Lizard." You may recall that, at Jesus' invitation, clumsy Peter "stepped out in faith" from his fishing boat and walked on the Sea of Galilee. Like the lizard, Peter stayed on the surface only as long as he didn't stop—stop focusing on Jesus, that is. When he looked around at the churning waters, his faith wavered like the waves that surged at his feet. He stopped looking at his water-borne Master and looked at the uncontrolled turbulence. Only at that point did he begin to sink, and called out to Jesus, in panic, to save him. Jesus lived up to his name—for Jesus means God Savior; he "reached out his hand and caught him" before Peter was completely submerged.

Jesus saw that it was time for a lesson, one to be taught in his typically incisive way—this time by a rebuke and a question: "You of little faith, why did you doubt?" (Mt 14:31). Peter's "little faith" was enough to make him venture forth on the water, but not enough to continue in the face of fear-bred doubt.

Like the water-skimming lizard, if we stop, we sink. Doubt stops the forward thrust of faith as a wall might stop a moving car. When facing problems, never stop facing the problem solver.

When You "Haven't the Foggiest," Look Again!

Airports close, ships collide, and cars crash when fog rolls in. But fog brings blessings too. Giant redwoods would die if they couldn't collect fog droplets, which drip moisture to their roots. The Scottish pine "feeds" off the fog, drawing essential minerals through its needles. The Welwitchia plant in the Namibian desert survives for rainless years only by waiting for a coastal fog to moisten its dry leaves. The tenebriond beetle drinks fog moisture collected on its back, and the dune beetle digs trenches perpendicular to the fog's wind to collect the precious droplets. The village of Chungungo, in the Andes Mountains, finds its only source of water in fog moisture trapped by huge mountainside nets dripping sixteen thousand gallons daily!

Our wondrous world is full of nature's good-news-bad-news activities. Lightning, volcanic eruptions, blizzards, earthquakes, and heat waves all seem treacherous. But they carry countless blessings for our great earth's general climate, environment, and incredibly delicate ecological balance.

Likewise, every personal "disaster"—from an ingrown toenail to terminal cancer, from a slight misunderstanding to a shattered marriage—is a good-news-bad-news event. The good news is: "The Lord works out everything for his own ends" (Prv 16:4) and also for our own good, in this life or the next. But this is only for those who love God, and thus try to conform to his will: "In *all* things God works for the good of those who love him" (Rom 8:28).

Uh-Oh—No Spaghetti-Os!

144 Oklahoma death row inmate Thomas Grasso requested for his last meal the popular canned pasta, Spaghetti-Os. When served plain spaghetti, he was enraged and threatened to notify the press.

As death nears, usually our value system begins to change. But persons who deny—or give no thought to—an afterlife, and especially an afterlife with a resurrected body, would do well to meditate on the words of Paul: "If the dead are not raised, 'Let us eat and drink, for tomorrow we die.' Do not be misled... Come back to your senses as you ought" (1 Cor 15:32-34).

Paul could identify with any death row inmate, for he was near death many times: "Indeed, in our hearts we felt the sentence of death. But this happened that we might not rely on ourselves but on God.... On him we have set our hope" (2 Cor 1:9-10). Imagine how Paul might respond to that death row inmate finicky about his last meal, with no hope or concern about life after death. "We do not want you to be ignorant [about death]... like the rest... who have no hope" (1 Thes 4:13). "If only for this life we have hope... we are to be pitied more than all men" (1 Cor 15:19).

With Paul, all of us who suffer might say, "I die every day" (15:31). But does that "daily death" make us eternity-focused?

Commuting Is for the Birds

A sparrow was strangely attracted to a car in Pittsford, New York. Through a small hole in the floorboard, it managed to build its nest and laid three eggs in the car's trunk. No one knows where the fledglings were hatched, because the owner of the car commuted forty miles each day, unaware of the nestlings in the trunk, who were somehow fed by the enterprising mother sparrow.

Imprinted into the tiny sparrow's brain is its incredibly complex, neurochemically based instinct, enabling it to adjust to varying surroundings (even adapting to a forty-mile daily commute!), and survive for unnumbered centuries as one of countless species.

Reminiscent of Jesus' teaching, there's a lesson here—and it's not for the birds, but for us worrisome children of a loving, provident Father. "Are not two sparrows sold for a penny? Yet not one of them will fall to the ground apart from the will of your Father.... You are worth more than many sparrows" (Mt 10:29, 31). "They do not sow or reap, they have no storeroom or barn; yet God feeds them. And how much more valuable you are than birds! Who of you by worrying can add a single hour to his life? Since you cannot do this very little thing, *why do you worry* about the rest?" (Lk 12:24-26; Mt 6:26-27).

That same God who spares sparrows lovingly takes care of you and me. So why should we worry? Let's simply "let go and let God."

Ladybug

146 In ancient Scandinavian mythology, Freya was the goddess of love and youth. Springtime, the season of love, was marked by swarms of colorful beetles, which therefore were regarded as "love messengers of Freya." Early Catholic missionaries strove to Christianize this pagan belief, redirecting the pagan cult of Freya to a devotional veneration of the Virgin Mary, by renaming the beetles "Our Lady's little birds." Later American colonists simplified that name to "ladybugs"—the name used by most today.

In my own fanciful piety as a child, I used to think that ladybugs were named for Our Lady—if you'll excuse a respectful pun—because Our Lady once "bugged" her Son, Jesus, at the wedding at Cana (see John 2), by simply hinting, "They have no wine." By that unaffected intercessory prayer she gently "bugged" him to work his first—and "unplanned"— miracle, changing water into wine to save the host embarrassment. And then she "bugged" the servants to do Jesus' will, not hers, as his instruments: "Do whatever he tells you." Even today she "bugs" us to do nothing but God's holy will.

Thirty-three years before the Cana episode, Mary herself, through the intermediary word of the Angel Gabriel, had been "bugged" by God to become the mother of the Incarnate Word. "The Mighty One" did great things for her, for which she would be called blessed for all generations (see Luke 1:48-49). And today Our Lady "bugs" us to live holy lives as his children—and hers.

When the Well Runs Dry

In one Western town, all customers with long-over-due water bills awoke one morning during a sweltering heat wave to find locked valves on their water inlets. With valves closed, wallets opened as if by magic, and the town's budget was finally balanced.

Most people will undergo almost any sacrifice to protect their own interests, when confronted with serious consequences. Only those with a true sense of responsibility will fulfill their obligations without having to be pressured by a threat.

God would prefer to have us act out of pure love for him and the desire to do his will perfectly, rather than to be motivated by fear of punishment. But for poorly motivated or irresponsible souls, the threat of punishment is required—like the shut-off of a water supply. Someone has said, "Many people get to heaven only by backing away from hell—a 'hell' of a way to get to heaven!"

As Paul and Barnabas reminded their hearers in Syria, "We must go through many hardships to enter the kingdom of God" (Acts 14:22). Whether these hardships entail suffering or simply obeying God's expressed will, Jesus tells us how to do it: "If anyone would come after me, he must *deny himself* and *take up his cross...* Whoever wants to save his life will lose it, but whoever loses his life for me will find it" (Mt 16:24-25). It's better to pay the bill on time than to wait until the water is shut off.

Blimey, It's a Limey

148 British sailors have traditionally been called "Limeys." The term originated in 1747, when Dr. James Lind proved experimentally that the antidote for the dreaded disease of scurvy was citrus fruits, like limes, which were usually not available on long sea voyages (the crucial element, vitamin C, was identified much later). Becoming "lime-eaters," the sailors were called "Limeys."

The statistics were overwhelming. More seamen died or were incapacitated from scurvy than from all other diseases, naval battles, marine mishaps, accidents, and shipwrecks combined. Dr. Lind's simple recommendation saved the lives of countless sailors.

For the varied problems that plague mankind, God's providence has provided simple remedies— many of which he has revealed. The most urgent ones are the spiritual problems, and the solutions for these include a wide range of such things as prayers of petition for healing or deliverance, faith, grace, Bible study, spiritual counseling, contrition, the sacraments and sacramentals, the use of charismatic gifts, and information from teaching and preaching. Certainly the solution for *any* spiritual problem is available; God's revelation has not left us in ignorance.

If you have an ongoing spiritual problem, then probably you're not using an available remedy—or not using it effectively. God's armamentarium is well stocked. Use it with deep gratitude.

Spare Ribs

One of the strangest anomalies puzzling geneticists today is the occurrence of an extra rib in sixteen percent of Eskimo men.

It seems, at times, that the Lord likes to give a little extra of some things—rather like a photographer that takes an extra picture of a group, "just in case." After Jesus fed the five thousand with five loaves and two fish, there were twelve baskets of food left over (see Mark 6:43). When he fed the four thousand with seven loaves and a few fish, there were seven basketfuls left over (see Matthew 15:37). Generosity is a characteristic of love; and God's abundance is the characteristic of his munificence, "that they may have life, and have it *to the full*" (Jn 10:10).

Our God is more than a God of sufficiency, he is a God of abundance. We have more air than we need to breathe, more food than we need to survive, more time than we need to become holy, more strength than we need to suffer, and more grace than we need to be saved. Our problem is that we don't make use of this superabundance as well as we could and should. In fact, we usually aren't even grateful and we waste it, not "collecting basketfuls."

Let us make our entire life a prayer of bountiful praise and thanksgiving for a bountiful God full of bountiful love for us!

Comeuppance for a Submarine

150 You've heard of persons being charged with reckless driving, but have you ever heard of anyone charged with reckless *diving*? The harbor patrol in Redondo Beach, California, lodged that charge against a man testing his invention there—a miniature submarine! Having neglected three previous warnings, he was finally ticketed with a citation and fine for "endangering surface craft by submerging and emerging in the vicinity of the harbor entrance."

Inconsideration for the welfare of others takes many forms. There are simple discourtesies, such as uncovered sneezing or littering on streets or in public restrooms. Sometimes we are merely thoughtless, like when we are habitually late in keeping appointments or constantly interrupt another's thoughts. Other, more blatant, offenses might include reckless driving—or diving!

Paul, who strove to please everyone in every way (see 1 Corinthians 10:33), said that "nobody should seek his own good but the good of others" (10:24). He tells us "to bear with the failings of the weak and not to please ourselves. Each of us should please his neighbor for his good, to build him up" (Rom 15:1-2), because love "is not rude, not self-seeking" (1 Cor 13:5). "Each of you," he says, "should look not only to your own interests, but also to the interests of others" (Phil 2:4). There's no greater challenge!

Other Helpful Resources by Father Hampsch

One Minute Sermons—by Phone

If you've read this book and would like more, you're in luck! "One Minute Sermons for Busy People" is now available by phone. Call 1-900-ALL-4-GOD (1-900-255-4465). At $1.99 per minute, these minute-long "snooze-proof sermonettes" could become a double source of blessing to you each week. How? "A big hunk of the phone bill payment automatically diverts to us here at CTM to help support our foreign missions," says Father Hampsch. "One call does it all–it feeds your spirit and feeds the poor at the same time!"

The Art of Loving God

The four stages of every person's spiritual journey are explored in this book. From "Back to Basics" to "Coping with Potholes, Pitfalls, and Panic," the wit and wisdom packed into these pages will both challenge Christians in their own spiritual growth and provide a useful tool to help others grow as well. **$8.99**

Books available at your Christian bookstore or from:
**Servant Publications * Dept. 209 * P.O. Box 7455
Ann Arbor, Michigan 48107**
Please include payment plus $2.75 per book
for postage and handling.
Send for our FREE catalog.